Grief Dreams

T. J. Wray
with Ann Back Price

Grief Dreams

How They Help Heal Us After the Death of a Loved One

JOSSEY-BASS
A Wiley Imprint
www.josseybass.com

Published by Jossey-Bass
A Wiley Imprint
989 Market Street, San Francisco, CA 94103-1741   www.josseybass.com

Jossey-Bass books and products are available through most bookstores. To contact Jossey-Bass directly call our Customer Care Department within the U.S. at 800-956-7739, outside the U.S. at 317-572-3986, or fax 317-572-4002.

Jossey-Bass also publishes its books in a variety of electronic formats. Some content that appears in print may not be available in electronic books.

The contents of this work are intended to further general scientific research, understanding, and discussion only and are not intended and should not be relied upon as recommending or promoting a specific method, diagnosis, or treatment by physicians or any other practitioners for any particular patient. The publisher and the author make no representations or warranties with respect to the accuracy or completeness of the contents of this work and specifically disclaim all warranties, including without limitation any implied warranties of fitness for a particular purpose. Readers should consult with a specialist where appropriate. The fact that an organization or Web site is referred to in this work as a citation and/or a potential source of further information does not mean that the author or the publisher endorses the information the organization or Web site may provide or recommendations it may make. Further, readers should be aware that Internet Web sites listed in this work may have changed or disappeared between when this work was written and when it is read. No warranty may be created or extended by any promotional statements for this work. Neither the publisher nor the author shall be liable for any damages arising herefrom. For the purpose of preserving anonymity and privacy, the names and identifying information of some persons whose stories are told in this book have been changed.

Library of Congress Cataloging-in-Publication Data
Wray, T. J.
  Grief dreams : how they help heal us after the death of a loved one /
[by T. J. Wray and Ann Back Price].
     p. cm.
  Includes bibliographical references.
  ISBN 0-7879-7678-4 (alk. paper)
  1. Death in dreams. 2. Grief. 3. Bereavement—Psychological aspects.
I. Price, Ann Back, date- II. Title.
  BF1099.D4W83 2005
  154.6'32—dc22   2004016534

Printed in the United States of America
FIRST EDITION
HB Printing   10 9 8 7 6 5 4 3 2 1

Contents

For Bob and Rosanne,
in memory of
Megan,
and
to all who mourn

Preface

Following the unexpected death of my only brother in 1997, I began work on a book about the unique grief experience of surviving adult siblings. In the process of writing *Surviving the Death of a Sibling: Living Through Grief When an Adult Brother or Sister Dies*, I had the opportunity to speak with thousands of bereaved siblings. During the course of most of these conversations, the subject of grief dreams invariably came up; it was the one topic everyone wanted to discuss. I also noticed that the topic of grief dreams seemed to surface frequently on the discussion board and during weekly chats at the adult sibling grief Web site (www.adultsiblinggrief.com).

Such conversations would often shift from dreams of deceased siblings to dreams of other deceased family members. I became fascinated with these dream stories and noted the healing effects they had in the lives of mourners. As I began to investigate this topic more thoroughly, I was surprised to find that very little had been written about the many benefits of grief dreams. I'm not sure why there hasn't been a greater focus on grief dreams in bereavement literature, but this book will surely help fill the gap.

Written in conjunction with Ann Back Price, a Jungian psychoanalyst and dream expert, *Grief Dreams* uses a relational approach. Through the shared dream stories of mourners who have lost cherished loved ones, *Grief Dreams* weaves together elements of psychology and spirituality so that readers will find some aspect of the book meaningful and helpful in their individual journey of loss.

Our underlying focus is not whether dreams are products of the unconscious or intentional visitations from beyond; rather, we believe dreams can be powerful tools that can actually help you navigate your personal journey of loss. In other words, *Grief Dreams* is designed to help mourners reclaim some measure of power during a time when they're probably feeling quite powerless.

We are sadly familiar with the pain and sorrow of grief in our own lives, having each suffered losses of beloved family members and treasured friends. But like many of those who contributed their grief dream stories to this book, we have found great consolation in our dreams. Those who contributed their dreams to this book expressed hope that their dream stories might help others cope with the loneliness, pain, and heartache of grief. We share in this hope. Indeed the central purpose of this book is to lend comfort and support to all those who mourn. (Although most contributors chose to use their real names, others preferred to use pseudonyms. And some details have been altered slightly to protect the identity of certain contributors.) This is not a psychoanalytical book. Nor is it intended to replace any form of grief therapy or psychological counseling, though it may serve to complement either.

In addition to reading this book, mourners are encouraged to visit our Web site, www.griefdreams.com. This site features information, message boards, a memorial page, chat, and other helpful features for those who wish to learn more about the nature of grief dreams or who simply want to share their dream experience with others.

Finally, whether your journey of grief is marked by days or decades, it is our shared hope that some measure of solace may be found in these pages.

ACKNOWLEDGMENTS

Together, we would like to thank our family, friends, and colleagues for their encouragement and support in this project. We'd also like to acknowledge Gary DiCasparro of Tec Direct for his computer expertise and Dave Castiglioni for his help with the grief dreams Web site (www.griefdreams.com). Special thanks to Rob McQuilkin of Lippincott, McQuilkin and Co. and Alan Rinzler of Jossey-Bass. Finally, we'd like to express our heartfelt gratitude to all of our wonderful contributors, whose dreams grace these pages and whose loved ones are herein memorialized.

Specific Acknowledgments from T. J. Wray

Special thanks to my husband, Rob, and children, Bob, Anne, and Jack; to my parents and siblings; and to all the wonderful Wrays for their understanding and love. Many thanks to the faculty, staff, and students of Salve Regina University, particularly the Religious Studies Department, and the members of the Adult Sibling Grief Peer Support Group, for their affirmation and support. Thanks, also, to Dr. Earl Thompson and Walter Burr for their guidance and friendship. And finally, I'd like to express my deep gratitude to all of my amazing women friends, who continue to grace my life with love and friendship, most especially, my indispensable friend and coauthor extraordinaire, Ann Back Price.

Specific Acknowledgments from Ann Back Price

I wish to thank my parents, Muriel and Robert Back, and my siblings, Martha, Rob, and Tim, for their faith and encouragement. I give my everlasting gratitude to my husband, Larry, my daughter, Laura Rose, and my son, Max Daniel, for their loving support and humor. To my Jungian and Brown colleagues, I am grateful for all I have learned. I am indebted to my friends (you know who you are) for affirmation and perspective. And most particularly I thank T. J. Wray: I am honored by our friendship and this experience.

T. J. Wray
Ann Back Price
Providence, Rhode Island

Introduction

Why a Book About Grief Dreams?

One of the most troubling aspects of grief is our sense of power-
lessness. Grieving people feel hopeless and frustrated because
nothing can be done to change the terrible events that resulted in
their present misery. Although it's true that there are few things that
can ease the suffering associated with profound loss, it *is* possible to
tap into the healing powers of our dreams. It's clear that most grieving
people find deep meaning and consolation in their dreams of deceased
loved ones. In fact, most mourners hope and pray for such dreams.

DREAMS CAN HEAL

Because grief dreams are a fairly universal phenomenon among the
bereaved, they offer the opportunity, when affirmed as important and
properly understood, for healing. Take the following, for example.

Katherine and David

"About four months after my fiancé, David, died," says Katherine,
"I began having dreams about him." Katherine recalls one particular dream—a visitation dream—that brought her a great deal of
comfort.

*In the dream, David is holding my hands in his. We are sitting close, side
by side. It is quiet. There is nothing else—no sound, no view—there is
feeling instead of seeing. There is just David and I.*

"I woke up from this dream feeling warm, protected, loved, and not alone," says Katherine as she revels in the positive and healing feelings her dream brings. "For a few moments, I forgot," she says. "I was in that special place between sleep and awake, when you don't remember, but love lives."

The Healing Power of Grief Dreams

Katherine is deeply consoled by her dreams of David. Grief dreams allow us to reconnect with our deceased loved ones, to return to that place where nothing has changed—a place where our loved one is still alive—a place where grief does not exist. In one incredible, magical moment, the chasm of death and despair evaporate, and we are given a few precious moments with our beloved. And herein lies the amazing power of the *grief dream*.

Grief dreams, moreover, can serve as gentle reminders that our loved one is still part of our life. And these dreams can help us in the painful adjustment process that is part of every grief journey. Finally, grief dreams allow us to transcend the limits of space and time and to have what every grieving person desires most: just one more visit.

TYPES OF GRIEF DREAMS

In attempting to understand the nature of grief dreams, it's helpful to recognize that most grief dreams fall into four rather broad categories:

- The visitation dream

- The message dream

- The reassurance dream

- The trauma dream

Of course, not all grief dreams fit into these specific categories. For example, some grief dreams may have elements of more than one dream type—such as a dream that is both a message dream *and* a reassurance dream. For clarity purposes, however, we'll focus on the four main grief dream types throughout most of this book. (See Chapter Seven for grief dreams that do not fall into the four main categories.)

Visitation Dreams

In the visitation dream, the dreamer merely spends time with the deceased. These dreams may recall a forgotten memory of the dreamer, sometimes from childhood. Often the dreamer reports that there was no prophetic message or warnings in the dream; rather, it was just a "final visit." Such visits may be quiet and pensive, or they might come in the form of joyous reunions, as Constance describes:

My daughter, Sarah, had been gone for almost a year when I had this dream. In the dream, she was sitting in the recliner in our living room. She was happy and excited to be home. I went to her, got down on my knees, and laid my head in her lap, crying for joy. I told her how happy I was that she was back, and she reached out and put her hand on my head.

The simple gesture of Sarah's healing touch brings comfort and solace to her grieving mother, and Constance considers this lovely visitation to be a special gift from her daughter.

Message Dreams

In the message dream, the dreamer receives some sort of important information, instruction, or even warning from the deceased. For example, your deceased cousin may appear in a dream and warn you to take better care of your health, or your father may appear in a dream to remind you not to work so hard. Message dreams are usually brief and overt. Sometimes the message is intended for someone other than the dreamer, as in the following:

I had this dream about three months after my grandmother died. In the dream, it is dark, but streetlights glow reassuringly, lighting my way. Up ahead is a bus stop, the kind with a Plexiglas-enclosed shelter and small bench inside. As I approach, my grandmother leans forward and peers out at me from around the enclosure. I am filled with happiness, relief, and joy. She hurries to me, takes my arm, and says, "I want you to tell your mother that I'm OK, that we're all OK. Can you do that?" I say, "Yes, I'll tell her." She releases my arm and walks away. As she leaves, she looks over her shoulder and says, "I have to go now. Don't forget to tell your mother." And then she is gone.

Christina wakes from this dream and counts down the hours until morning, eager to share her grandmother's uplifting message with her mother. "We've had a lot of loss in our family," she says, "and this dream helped all of us to feel more hopeful."

Reassurance Dreams

The reassurance dream is a consoling dream that encourages the dreamer to take comfort. Quite often, the deceased gives the dreamer some much needed affirmation that he or she is doing a good job or doing the right thing in a particular area of life. Sometimes, as in the following reassurance dream, the deceased tells the dreamer not to worry because he or she is doing well in the afterlife.

I had this dream about my best friend, Paula, about six months after she died in a car accident. The dream began in a huge, dark room, but I was not scared. At the far end of the room, I saw soft, beautiful white light and Paula floating out of the light and coming toward me. She had one arm extended to me and she was smiling. I was so happy and excited— I wanted to run to her, but I couldn't move. I began to cry and told her how much I missed her. She continued to smile, and she told me that everything was all right and that she missed me, too. Slowly, she receded and I woke up.

Ellen wakes from this dream with tears of joy streaming down her face. "I felt happy and content, as if I got to say good-bye to her," she says. "It felt good to tell her how much I missed her."

Time Travelers wife

Trauma Dreams

The most disturbing grief dream is the trauma dream. Less common than the other types of grief dreams, the trauma dream often comes in the form of a flashback, especially in early grief and particularly in cases of traumatic deaths, such as murders, suicides, and accidents. Many times, the dreamer feels powerless and afraid, as in the following trauma dream.

I had this dream about five months after my uncle's sudden and unexpected death. In the dream, a thunderstorm was raging. High winds had knocked over a swing set—minus the swings—onto my Uncle Ritchie's lower legs, just above the ankles. He was pinned down and struggling to get up. The dream ended with me rushing through the storm, intending to lift the swing set off of him.

Bobbie describes this dream as a nightmare. "I awoke from this dream crying and feeling scared," she says. "I had had other nightmares that same night, but this one was the only one I could remember." Yet, despite the feelings of fear and dread that this dream brings, over time, Bobbie comes to view the dream as healing. "When I wrote about this dream in my dream journal," she says, "I was strangely comforted. It was healing to simply write about my uncle, to remember him."

HOW TO READ THIS BOOK

Grief Dreams is arranged in a logical, easy-to-read fashion, with the four categories of grief dreams forming the core of the book. In these core chapters (Chapters Three through Six), a variety of grief dreams are presented—actual dreams from grieving people, just like you. Dream symbols and other important features of each dream are discussed and deciphered. Every dream narrative is followed by a "back story," in which you can learn more about the relationship between the dreamer and the deceased. You may see elements of your own dreams and relationships in the variety of narratives presented.

How the Dream Stories Can Help You

The dream stories included in this book are designed both to affirm the importance of the dreams we have during bereavement and to offer hope and healing to all those who mourn. In addition, the dream stories actually become instruction tools for you, the reader, to gain insight and healing from your own grief dreams.

Following each dream story is a *Toolbox*, designed to assist the reader in interpreting his or her own dreams. The Toolboxes gradually increase in detail and complexity, and each new chapter will build on the last. Our goal is to bring the reader along slowly so that you can gain the confidence necessary to interpret your dreams. This confidence is enhanced by the easy-to-learn methods of interpretation that center on the concept that *you*, the dreamer, are in the best position to accurately interpret your own dreams. After all, your dreams are as unique as you are.

The Rest of the Book

Although best read from cover to cover, *Grief Dreams* is designed so that mourners can turn to a specific chapter that addresses their particular dream type. In addition to the four core chapters (Three through Six) that center on the main categories of grief dreams, there are other supporting chapters: Chapters One and Two explore both the grief process and the dream process. They provide the necessary background for a better understanding of all subsequent chapters. Chapter Seven focuses on grief dreams that do not seem to fit into the standard four categories. Chapter Eight explores the connections between faith and grief and the religious images found in grief dreams. And Chapter Nine addresses the ways in which grief dreams can help heal the pain of loss. It also includes questions about seeking professional help. Extensive Reader Resources and Selected Sources sections conclude the book.

Beyond understanding the various grief dream types, beyond the dream detective work, and beyond the sheer joy that mourners feel in being reunited with loved ones, there is something more powerful at work in grief dreams: our grief dreams can actually help heal us. And that is what *Grief Dreams* is all about.

1

The Journey of Grief

The presence of that absence is everywhere.
Edna St. Vincent Millay

The first glimmers of dawn herald the start of a new day. Parents rustle their children from slumber; coffee shops begin to fill up with businesspeople in need of their morning lattes; cars, buses, and trains carry the masses to various destinations. As the world wakes up, thousands of red-rimmed eyes watch from thousands of windows, wondering how it can be that the sun should dare to shine—or that people should care about lattes or rush hours. For the grieving person, the hum of daily human activity seems blasphemous. Don't they know? Haven't they heard? My loved one is gone and nothing will ever be the same again.

Grief is a nightmare you have when you're awake.

Several years ago, Donna lost her only son. A healthy high school sophomore, Tommy died as he sat in front of his computer, doing homework. Although no definite cause of death was ever determined, an undiagnosed heart ailment seemed the likely culprit. Donna's life of enviable normality suddenly, and without warning, disappeared and was replaced by a life of pain, heartache, and uncertainty.

A few weeks after her son's death, when asked by a friend how she was coping, Donna replied, "Grief is a nightmare you have when you're awake."

Like Donna, many grieving people agree that there is often a surreal, nightmarish quality associated with grief. Our thoughts and movements are sluggish; we're sometimes consumed with an overwhelming sense of dread; and our search for escape is usually in vain. In early grief, there is often a detached sensation, as if we are merely observing some strange drama from a distance. After all, this can't really be happening; this can't be real.

But it is real.

Although the analogy of a nightmare may be *one* way to describe grief, clinical descriptions of grief usually include words like *acute sorrow* or *deep distress*. But most grieving people find that clinical definitions fail to capture the emotional depths and diverse reactions we experience after losing someone we love. So what exactly are we talking about when we speak of grief? Are there any universal reactions to this nearly universal experience?

THE EXPERIENCE OF GRIEF

Even though each person's journey of grief differs—and in the same person, the reaction to each new loss will also differ—there are some general observations about grief that can be helpful in trying to understand how we grieve.

Emotional and Physical Pain

First, we know that for most mourners, grief can be both emotionally and physically painful. Emotional reactions may include disbelief, deep sadness, anger, and depressed mood. Many mourners also report feeling confused and disoriented; a distorted sense of time is also common, particularly in early grief.

In addition to the emotional reactions associated with grief, there are also physical symptoms, ranging from shakiness, nausea, shortness of breath, sighing, dizziness, and general weakness to fainting, chest pain, and even an inability to speak. Although such physical symptoms are more common in early grief, it is not at all uncommon to experience physical reactions alongside the emotional reactions at any time during the grief process.

It's also important to point out that there may be a marked absence of these emotional and physical symptoms. But the absence of what many consider to be "typical grief behaviors," such as crying or depression, does not mean that a person isn't grieving. Indeed we all grieve in our own particular way. In bereaved families, for example, each family member will react differently to his or her loss. Some may be more overt in their grief, and others, more circumspect.

Sense of Loss

Second, when we grieve, it is always in the context of being the one "left behind." Grief, of course, can result from a variety of losses (for example, the loss of a job promotion, the dissolution of a relationship, the realization that a trust has been betrayed), but the focus of this book is the grief associated with the death of a loved one. Of course, all losses mean that the cherished person (or thing) is no longer there—and that we are left behind to mourn the loss.

In most cases, grief is a normal, healthy response to the death of someone you love. Contrary to popular belief, there are no timetables and no rules of the road for grief. And, generally speaking, those who love deeply tend to grieve deeply. So there's nothing abnormal about feeling the pain of loss, even for many years or even for a lifetime.

Beginning of a Journey

Finally, grief seems to have a progressive movement associated with it—ranging from immobilizing despondency to functioning acceptance. Because grief tends to shift and change over time, grief experts often describe it as a *process* or a *journey*.

Elisabeth Kübler-Ross was among the first to explore dying and grief in terms of stages: stage one—*shock, denial, and isolation,* stage two—*anger*, stage three—*bargaining*, stage four—*depression*, stage five—*acceptance*. Since Kübler-Ross's initial work, many others have put forth their own models in an effort to describe the process of grief.

Models can be immensely helpful in trying to understand what happens to us when we grieve, but it's also important to remember that even though you may experience some of the reactions outlined in the various models, grief is a highly individual process. Indeed your personal journey of grief is as unique as you are.

Still, words like *models*, *stages*, *phases*, *symptoms*, and *reactions* are important because they provide a language, a way of speaking about grief as *a process*. In reviewing the various grief theories, and in our many conversations with the bereaved, we have come to understand grief as a fluid, rather than a linear, process. And we have observed three very general phases of grief, which will serve as a way of thinking about and discussing grief throughout this book.

- *Phase one: disbelief*. This is most common in early grief and is characterized by shock, numbness, denial, and withdrawal.

- *Phase two: disarray*. The mourner feels a sense of emotional upheaval. This phase includes a variety of emotions, including anger, fear, worry, and depression.

- *Phase three: denouement*. This is characterized by acceptance, adjustment, reconnecting with others, and the search for meaning.

If you are in the midst of early grief—or even if your loss is less recent but you find that you are having a difficult time coping—knowing what to expect and having some tools at your disposal will help you as you move forward on your journey of loss. What follows is a general discussion of some of the reactions associated with grief. This discussion is framed using the three phases just outlined and is followed by suggestions (in the Toolbox) that may help you better cope with your loss. Because grief is not a "one-size-fits-all" process, you will naturally find some suggestions more helpful than others.

PHASE ONE: DISBELIEF

Some of the emotions typically associated with early grief may include but are not limited to shock, numbness, denial, and withdrawal. Mourners may vacillate between all of these emotions or may experience something entirely different.

Shock and Numbness

In general, most people experience some form of shock or numbness upon receiving the news that their loved one has died. These feelings may last for a few moments, for days, or even for weeks and may disappear only to resurface at a later time. All of this can also be said of most emotions associated with grief.

"I'll never forget that phone call," says Robert. "My father called me at work and told me that my mother passed away in her sleep after suffering a stroke. I felt dazed. I couldn't believe it. I couldn't move. I think I stopped breathing."

Robert accurately captures many of the feelings often associated with disbelief. The news of his mother's death is shocking, and he is overcome with a paralyzing sense of incredulity.

Like Robert, Beth is at work when she learns of her father's sudden death from a fatal heart attack. "At first, I was in shock. Just completely stunned," says Beth after receiving the fateful phone call from her older brother. "But then, I felt numb—shut down—like I was no longer a part of my own body," she says. Beth describes this numbness as a sort of disengagement from the real world, where she *appears* to be functioning normally, but in reality, she's operating on autopilot. "During those first few days, I went through the motions like a robot. I even went back to work the day after Dad died, although I certainly wasn't very productive. Everyone was amazed.

They crept past my office door, not knowing what to say," she recalls.

Although Beth's return to the office so soon after her father's death may seem premature to some, this sort of grief response is actually quite common. Like many mourners, Beth is suddenly cast into a sea of grief and must now navigate the turbulent waters of loss in her own way. Work becomes Beth's life preserver, a familiar and secure place in her new and unpredictable world of grief.

Like Beth, each of us will react and cope with our loved one's death in our own unique way. Some may react with shock, numbness, stunned silence, or uncontrolled hysteria, whereas others may appear to have little or no outward reaction at all.

How each of us reacts to such news is determined by a variety of factors, including differences in our particular personalities, whether or not others are around to offer us support, and the nature of the relationship we shared with the deceased.

Anticipated or Unanticipated Death

Often the cause of death determines much of our initial reactions. For example, if your loved one passes away after a long battle with cancer, the death is classified as an *anticipated death*, which means that you knew that your loved one was dying. With anticipated deaths, friends and family members often begin the grieving process while their loved one is still alive. They have time to imagine what life will be like without their loved one, and often they are able to share meaningful moments together that can ease the pain of impending separation for both.

Mourners often report that they felt better in having some time to prepare for their loved one's passing. Although this preparation time can be quite helpful for some, this is not always the case. "I knew my Uncle John was dying," says Carrie. "And I thought I had prepared myself for losing him. But when my mother called and gave me the news, I lost it. I guess I wasn't really prepared at all."

Generally speaking, however, the initial reactions associated with an anticipated death are likely to differ from the reactions associated with a sudden or *unanticipated death*. Unanticipated deaths occur without warning, such as deaths resulting from accidents, homicides, or suicides. Because the death is unexpected, most people report an overwhelming sense of shock and denial.

"I just couldn't believe it," says Debbie. "My nephew was at my house watching the game with my husband and me. He was killed in a car accident involving a drunk driver on the way back to his apartment. I was in complete shock. I didn't know what to do."

In addition to the shock associated with unanticipated deaths, mourners often express guilt, regret, or anger because they did not have the opportunity to say good-bye, to express love, to ask for or offer forgiveness. All of this naturally intensifies grief.

Denial

In early grief, the feelings of shock or numbness often give way to an overwhelming sense of denial. Most grief experts describe denial as a psychological coping mechanism that allows our minds to gradually absorb the magnitude of our loss. At first, denial of the death itself is common. For example, when the doctor informed Sally that her grandmother died, Sally wondered if perhaps the doctor had made a mistake. "Are you sure it was my grandmother?" she asked, suspiciously. "Perhaps you have the wrong woman. My grandmother wasn't that sick!"

When Michael's mother told him of the auto accident that claimed his father's life, Michael immediately created a false scenario of events in his head: his father's car and wallet were stolen by a crazed carjacker who then crashed his father's car. Dad isn't *really* dead; he's probably wandering around the countryside somewhere, looking for a pay phone to call home.

Although for most the phase of denial is short-lived, many grieving people report a more prolonged sense of denial. For instance,

Norma, a bereaved sibling, made a conscious choice to deny her sister's death: "Because my sister and I lived in different states, it was easy for me to pretend she was still alive since we rarely saw each other anyway."

It's important to mention that the sort of denial associated with grief—whether it is brief or prolonged—is usually not a symptom of some deeper illness. In fact, denial can serve an important emotional (and practical) purpose. For example, denial can help cushion the impact of our loss so that we can plan and attend our loved one's funeral. In fact, it is usually a heavy dose of denial that helps us move through those first difficult days and weeks following our loved one's death.

Of course, denial's protective anesthetic will eventually wear off. This may happen all at once, or little by little, but one thing is for certain: once the veil of denial has been lifted, the real work of grief begins.

Need for Solitude

As shock and denial fade into the horrible reality of the permanence of death, grief hovers on the edge of every thought, every action, and every suffocating breath. Although at this point, you may have already returned to work or at least attempted to resume some aspects of the routine that marked your life before your loss, you're probably finding it difficult to be around others. Your home, your office, your friends and coworkers—all appear unchanged. This should be comforting to you, but it's not—because *you* have changed.

Life is suddenly unpredictable. Mourners never really know how they'll be feeling from one moment to the next because grief has a way of invading even the most mundane moments in life. One moment, you're standing in line at the bank, and the next, you're rushing out the door in tears after being ambushed by a sudden attack of grief. One moment, you're peeling potatoes over the sink, and the next, you're huddled on the couch, sobbing into a toss pillow, ambushed again. Grief respects no social conventions and knows no boundaries. Grief just is.

So it's no wonder many grieving people find that the consolation initially found in being surrounded by loved ones may instead be found in moments of solitude. Sometimes, when we're hurting, we simply need to withdraw for a time to try to make sense of things. This can be a healing time of sustained introspection, or it may simply reflect an inner need for silence.

"Everyone kept asking me how I was doing and if there was anything I needed," says Ben after his best friend passed away suddenly. "All I really wanted was some quiet time alone."

The need for solitude may or may not be part of your grief journey, but if it is, be warned that those around you may express concern. "Megan sits for long periods of time in her room just listening to music," says her mother. "Her little poodle, Tasha, died two weeks ago, and Megan has suddenly withdrawn from the rest of the family."

Your need to withdraw is often confusing to others, because the desire to be alone doesn't mean that you no longer need the support of your friends and family. This, of course, is somewhat of a paradox: you want to be alone, but you don't want to be abandoned. People have a way of reaching out and demonstrating great kindness when they first learn of your loss (often when you're already anesthetized by shock and denial), but after a few weeks, most people quickly forget that you're still grieving at precisely the time when the full impact of your loss really hits you.

To complicate matters, Americans are fairly inept when it comes to grief and condolence. This means, in most cases, that not only will those around you fail to do or say the right thing (or worse, they don't say or do *anything*), but you may not know how to ask for the kind of support you need.

Some mourners may not have any close friends or family members to whom they can turn for consolation. For example, if you were raised in a family that discouraged the sharing of deep feelings, or if you are new to a city and haven't yet made many friends, then you may literally have no place to go with your grief. You may feel your only option is to ignore your feelings, but in reality, that is probably the worst thing you can do.

The failure to deal with the death of a loved one can lead to something that psychologists call *complicated bereavement*. This means that you've crossed the line from a grief that is a normal, healthy reaction to the death of a loved one to a more pathological condition that requires medical care. Grief will not simply go away just because you're not dealing with it. It will surface and demand attention, often at inappropriate times, so it's best to deal with it now.

Toolbox: Managing Phase One

Despite the pain that comes with losing someone you love, there are a few things you can do to help yourself though the mire and misery of early grief.

1. Take care of your body. Eat, drink lots of fluids, and get a full night's sleep, if you're able. In early grief, it's fairly normal to neglect these things, but in doing so, you'll only feel worse.

2. Get into the habit of writing things down. Grieving people often find it difficult to concentrate and remember things like meetings and doctors' appointments. Because your life feels so confusing right now, it's important to reclaim some measure of order. Keeping a small notebook or date book handy and referring to it on a daily basis will help you feel less disconnected to the nongrieving world.

3. Be very clear in communicating your needs to others. For example, if you just don't feel up to large family gatherings right now or if you need more time alone, make certain that

those around you understand and respect your wishes. "Thanks for the offer, but I'm really not ready to be in large groups yet" is a sufficient response to an invitation you're not ready to accept. Don't feel as if you need to justify your feelings during this time. If you don't think you can handle certain social gatherings, just be honest. Most people will be sympathetic and understanding.

4. Consider engaging a grief partner. Grief partners are usually caring, compassionate people who are able and willing to act as a consoling and listening presence. This person can be a trusted friend, family member, neighbor, church member, or coworker.

Once you identify someone that you think could fulfill this important role, simply ask that person if he or she would be willing to help you through this difficult phase of your life. People who love and care about you are usually eager to do something to help ease your suffering. Without question, having a support person to help you navigate those first few weeks and months of grief is the single best step you can take to help yourself better cope with your loss.

PHASE TWO: DISARRAY

As mourners move from the world of disbelief, they step into a strange, new world. This world *resembles* the one you left behind when you learned of your loved one's death, but it is not the same. This new world is more like a battlefield, littered with land mines that can explode without warning. Chaos and confusion have replaced predictability. This is the world of disarray.

Although there are many emotions associated with this particular phase of grief, the two most common are anger (which also includes fear and worry) and depression.

Anger

When her roommate died from an accidental drug overdose, Courtney was furious. "I can't believe she would be so stupid!" Courtney
raged. "Everyone knows that taking that much ecstasy is dangerous!
What a waste." Like Courtney, most grieving people—though certainly not all—experience some form of anger, especially during the
first few months after losing a loved one.

Grief-related anger comes in many forms. For example, Courtney's anger is focused on the manner of death—a death she feels
could have been prevented. If your husband died of cancer, you may
feel angry about the fact that he didn't catch the cancer early
enough to be cured or that the doctors didn't do enough to save
him. If your cousin died in a motorcycle accident, you might feel
anger because the motorist who caused the accident wasn't more
careful, or perhaps your anger is directed at your cousin for not wearing a helmet. And, of course, when we lose someone we love, we
usually feel cheated, singled out for misery, and betrayed by God.
How could God allow this to happen? All of these types of anger
question the preventability of the death.

Deaths resulting from murder or suicide often result in more
intense feelings of anger. If your child was murdered, you may feel
anger at law enforcement for not keeping murderers in jail or for
failing to solve the case, anger at your child for not being more careful, anger at the killer for taking your child's life, and anger at yourself for not being able to protect her.

If your best friend commits suicide, you may feel a great deal of
anger at him for intentionally doing something that resulted in so
much grief, anger at yourself for not picking up the telltale signs of
depression, and anger at the situation that drove him to such an ex-
treme act.

And in most deaths, regardless of the circumstances, it is common to direct your anger at friends, family, and coworkers who failed

to affirm and recognize the depth of your loss. "No one seems to understand that just because I'm back to work, it doesn't mean that I'm back to normal," says Jim after his wife died. Jim feels angry at the way in which his coworkers have carefully avoided mentioning his wife in conversations and how some have even hinted that Jim should start dating again.

Fear and Worry

Anger may also appear wearing the costume of fear and worry. In fact, most grief experts note that anger is almost always connected to fear—and fear can lead to worry. During periods of intense grief, you may find that you experience many of the same symptoms you would typically associate with fear. C. S. Lewis, in his book *A Grief Observed* (p. 1), captures this reality best:

> No one ever told me that grief felt so much like fear.
> I am not afraid, but the sensation is like being afraid. The same fluttering in the stomach, the same restlessness.

Such fear often manifests in the form of worry. "After I lost my brother," says Jayne, "I suddenly became a worrier. I worried obsessively about my children becoming ill or being kidnapped, worried that my husband would die in a plane crash as he traveled on one of his business trips, and worried that my mother would simply die in her sleep of a broken heart." So fear and worry really come from the same place: anger.

Although you may intellectually understand that anger can be part of the grief process, you may nonetheless feel ill prepared to deal with it. Women, especially, often have a difficult time expressing anger because they have been socialized to "be nice." Men, in contrast, often express anger in inappropriate ways, such as through the use of physical force. It stands to reason that if we don't know how to express our anger under normal circumstances, we're not going to do much better when we're grieving.

Depression

In addition to anger, fear, and worry, most grieving people experience some form of depressed mood following the death of a loved one.

Debra, for example, is concerned about her mother. "Ever since Dad died, Mom's been really depressed. She used to love to go to the casino, but lately, all she does is sit on the sofa and watch game shows." Debra is worried about the changes in her mother's behavior and wonders if these changes are a normal part of the grief process. Debra has read about depression, particularly among the elderly, and she's concerned that her mother may need professional help. Even though a depressed mood is perhaps the most common emotion associated with grief, is that low mood technically a *depression?*

Actually, there is a difference between the depressed mood associated with grief and major depression. Bereavement author Alan Wolfelt helps draw a distinction between the two. According to Wolfelt, in normal grief, people usually respond to offers of support and comfort; in major depression, these offers of support are often refused. In normal grief, the bereaved are often openly angry; in major depression, a person may be irritable and might complain but represses his or her anger. In normal grief, the depression is directly related to the loss; in major depression, the depression is more generalized. In normal grief, mourners are still able to experience moments of enjoyment; in major depression, there is an absence of joy. Finally, in normal grief, transient physical problems and feelings of guilt over some specific aspect of the loss are common; in major depression, chronic physical complaints and a more generalized feeling of guilt are the norm.

Even though it's normal to feel some level of depression after the death of a loved one, grief-related depression can evolve into a more serious form of major depression. All depression symptoms therefore must be taken seriously and reported to your health care provider. The change from grief-related depression to a more serious type of depression can happen rather quickly. You should be diligent in monitoring all symptoms and report changes immediately to your physician. (See Chapter Nine and the Reader Resources section for more information on depression and seeking professional help.)

Toolbox: Managing Phase Two

Phase Two is often described as the most intense, prolonged phase of grief. Even though anger, fear, worry, and depression are normal aspects of grief, many mourners find it difficult to cope with such strong emotions. What follows are some possible strategies for dealing with disarray.

1. If you haven't yet done so, consider engaging a grief partner. Sometimes just having a sympathetic ear can be helpful in diffusing anger, reducing fear and worry, and easing the symptoms of depression.

2. Start a grief journal. Having a place where you can record your feelings can be enormously helpful. Your journal can be your safe place to vent, and it can also serve as a helpful tool in monitoring symptoms of depression.

3. Investigate the possibility of joining a grief support group. There's nothing like sharing your feelings with others who can truly relate to your feelings of grief. When possible, try to find a loss-specific support group, one that is composed of members who share similar losses. For example, if you've suffered the loss of a child, a group dedicated to bereaved parents will probably be most helpful to you.

Even among parent groups, however, there is a diverse population. If you lose a child in infancy, your grief is likely to differ from the grief of a parent who loses a teenager or an adult child. If possible, try to locate a group that addresses your particular type of loss. It may be difficult to find a loss-specific group, especially in rural areas. In that case, a general grief support group is usually better than gutting it out on your own. Of course, if you really aren't comfortable with the idea of a support group, you might consider one-on-one grief counseling. (See Chapter Nine and the Reader Resources section for more information on depression and seeking professional help.)

4. Begin a program of moderate physical exercise, such as walking, or meditative practices, such as yoga. You might bristle at the idea of getting out of the house and taking a walk when you're feeling so bereft, but physical activity not only helps defuse some of the anger you may be feeling, but it also helps with grief-related depression.

5. Learn to communicate your feelings to others. Those who love and care about you sincerely want to help you through this sad time, but it's up to you to let them know how they can best assist you. For example, if you're feeling fearful or worried about your teenager driving to a friend's house at night, ask your child to phone you once he or she has arrived. Let your child know the source of your worry and fear and enlist his or her support by saying something like, "Ever since Grandpa passed away, I worry a little more than I should. Please help me through this by phoning me so that I know that you've arrived safely."

6. Know your "triggers." Grief triggers are the people, places, and things that seem to exacerbate your feelings of anger, fear, worry, or depression. Avoiding those who trigger feelings of anger—such as those who have not been supportive to you or who have minimized your grief and chastised you for not "get-

ting on with your life"—is probably a good idea. Of course, there are some triggers that cannot be avoided. For example, the approach of an anniversary date, such as your loved one's birthday or death date, often acts as a trigger for depression. Anniversaries are inevitable, so try to anticipate and prepare for them as much as possible.

7. Educate yourself about depression. Your local mental health facility and library, as well as on-line resources, are the best places to begin. (See the Reader Resources section at the end of this book.) Most of these resources will be helpful in describing depression and offering strategies for coping with it.

8. Reach out to others. Identify those friends, family members, and coworkers who are understanding and sympathetic. Remind yourself that although you may feel alone in your sorrow, you *do* have a circle of loved ones who care.

PHASE THREE: DENOUEMENT

The word *denouement* is from the French, meaning to "untie." During this phase, the knot of grief is loosened, and we begin the process of rebuilding our lives. Eventually, we will untie the knot and examine the strands in new and different ways. Adjustments are often necessary in order to prevent the strands from reknotting, even though this is bound to happen from time to time.

Reconnecting

As we work one sort of knot free, however, we seek to establish another. During this phase, we work to reestablish ties, reconnecting with old friends and family members who have stood patiently on the sidelines of our grief journey. We may make dinner plans, look forward to family gatherings, and ever so slowly feel the small sparks of joy creeping back into our lives again.

Important work or old hobbies that have been shelved during the long dark days of intense bereavement are rediscovered, dusted off, and slowly integrated back into our lives. "Hal had been gone for almost a year before I started knitting again," says Millie. "Holding those knitting needles between my fingers after all that time was like having tea with an old friend."

Acceptance and Adjustment

Reconnecting with others, finding joy in life again, and resuming some of the activities we once enjoyed herald a change in our journey of grief. Some grief experts refer to this change as *acceptance* or *resolution*, which usually means that the mourner has in some way been released from an emotional attachment to the deceased. Most mourners would argue that such a detachment is neither their goal nor their desire. After all, love survives even the pain of death, making detachment impossible.

Acceptance can best be understood in terms of change and growth. You'll see signs of this growth as the periods of acute grief gradually diminish; eventually, you'll begin to have periods of time when you're not actively mourning. "In the beginning, I thought about Tom's death constantly," says Elaine. "But now, almost a year later, there are days when I don't think about it for hours at a time."

Elaine has begun to adjust to life without her husband; she has had to learn new skills and new ways of living in the world without him. For example, she has learned to mow the lawn, pay the bills, and take the car in for oil changes every few months, tasks formerly assigned to her husband. But beyond these practical adjustments, Elaine has begun to imagine a future that does not include Tom. The trips they had planned to take together, the grandchildren they had hoped to spoil together, and the dream of a retirement home in Florida must now be readjusted into new visions of the future.

We, too, must make certain adjustments as we transition from disarray to denouement. Bereavement author Thomas Attig observes that this is a transition from "loving in presence" to "loving in absence." But making this transition, and untying the knot of intense grief, does not mean that the pain of loss will magically come to an end. Indeed grief is not something from which we will someday be "cured." The truth is, grief changes us—we'll never be the same person we were before we experienced the death of someone we love. Once we accept this fact, the task of grief—the key to keeping the knot smooth—is to find meaning in our loss.

Finding Meaning

Meaning may include such things as personal growth or spiritual awakening, or it may be something more tangible, such as establishing a scholarship in your loved one's name or creating a square for the AIDS quilt.

When Susan lost two daughters—one to adoption and the other, many years later, to leukemia—she decided to write a book about her experiences. Susan also speaks publicly about her losses to adoption and bereavement groups and finds a great deal of meaning in these talks. "When I am able to help other bereaved parents who have lost children, either through adoption or death, it gives deeper meaning to my own losses. I think when I can help others to heal, I heal a little, too." Susan's work is an excellent example of successful meaning making.

Meaning, of course, will be different for each of us, and the way in which we search for and discover meaning may be as simple as recognizing the places where our loved one continues to live on—particularly in those we love. Of course, finding meaning does not signal an end to mourning. But it does mean that you have come to a place where you have incorporated the loss into your life, a place of acceptance and ultimately peace.

Toolbox: Managing Phase Three

The key to untying the knot of acute grief is through finding meaning in your loss. The following are some possible meaning-making activities that may assist you in your search for meaning.

1. Create a living memorial for your loved one. This can be something as simple as planting a single tree or something as major as designing a whole flower garden.

2. Put together a scrapbook of your loved one's life. Include such things as photographs, letters, awards, poetry, or stories that he or she may have written, anything that you feel helps define who your loved one was as a person. Share your finished creation with family and friends. You might also consider collaborating with others to make the scrapbook a group effort.

3. Create a video memorial, set to music of your choosing. Video memorials include photographs and film clips chronicling your loved one's life. These lovely, moving tributes can be shared with friends and family to commemorate a special event, such as your loved one's birthday. You don't need to purchase fancy software to do this. There are several companies that specialize in video memorials. See the Reader Resources section for details.

4. Devote your time and energy to a particular organization or cause. For example, if your mother died of breast cancer, you might organize a local group for the annual Making Strides Against Breast Cancer walk. If your best friend died in a car accident at a dangerous intersection, petition your town to install a traffic light to prevent future fatalities.

Now that you have a basic understanding of grief as a process or journey, it is equally important to have a general understanding of dreams. Chapter Two will provide some much needed information about dreams: how and why we dream and the role dreams play in waking life. Subsequent chapters will draw on Chapters One and Two as we explore the various types of grief dreams, including ways for you to find meaning in your own dreams.

As you move forward through these pages, it is important to keep in mind that your personal odyssey of grief is as unique as your dreams. This means that *you* are in the best position to both articulate your feelings of grief and give meaning to your dreams.

Remember, too, that you do not journey the path of grief alone. Others who have traveled this path before you will help you unlock the healing powers of your grief dreams.

2

About Dreams

Romeo: *I dreamt a dream to-night.*
Mercutio: *And so did I.*
Romeo: *Well, what was yours?*
                                   William Shakespeare, Romeo and Juliet

I had the weirdest dream last night," fifteen-year-old Laura announces to the car pool while driving to school one morning. "Yeah, I had one too," ventures Sarah, a quiet girl by the window. Laura prompts, "Mine was amazing. We were back in our old house, like we had never moved. What was yours?" Sarah muses, "I dreamt I was with my grandma again. She was brushing my hair and telling me stories, just like she used to before she died. It was so real, like she was really there."

Dreams spark our interest and kindle conversations in car pools, at parties, by the water cooler, over coffee, under the stars, and whenever we take a moment to reflect. Since the beginning of time, humans have valued their dreams. Ancient civilizations looked to dreams as a way to predict the future and to contact ancestors. Biblical dreams were understood as messages from God. In more recent history, musicians, artists, and scientists have credited their dreams for their inspiration. And in the field of modern psychology, the study of dreams has become an important aspect of therapeutic practice.

SIGMUND FREUD

In 1900, Sigmund Freud's landmark book *The Interpretation of Dreams* secured the analysis of dreams as a respected field of psychological study. Subsequently, C. G. Jung and others utilized the healing function of dreams as tools for personal growth. Although Freud and Jung were contemporaries who shared a fascination for the study of the unconscious, they developed opposing theories of the human mind and dream interpretation. The following discussion is a brief synopsis of Freudian and Jungian dream theory.

Dreams as Wish Fulfillments

Freud observed that dreams are the "royal road" to the *unconscious*. He held that dreams are *wish fulfillments*. Through the process of psychoanalysis, these repressed desires, usually of a sexual nature, could be uncovered. Freud believed that dreams had a *manifest content*, or surface meaning, that must be decoded in order to discover the hidden meaning, or *latent content*, of the dream. He worked with the dreamer, using *free association*, a process by which the dreamer was to say whatever came to mind when thinking about the various parts of a particular dream. The idea was that deep or hidden thoughts would eventually surface to help reveal the latent content of the dream, which Freud usually viewed within the context of sexuality. Of course, uncovering the latent meaning of a particular dream was often a difficult and time-consuming effort.

In *The Interpretation of Dreams*, Freud analyzed many of his own dreams using free association, including the often-cited dream of his patient Irma (dream of July 23–24, 1895). In his introduction, Freud revealed his concern that he had not entirely cured Irma. In his elegant interpretation (which included an explanation of Irma's repressed sexuality), Freud explained how the dream was the fulfillment of his own wish that he would not be blamed for Irma's suffering: "The dream represents a certain state of affairs such as I might wish to exist" (p. 205).

The Protective Function of Dreams

Freud also believed that the primary function of dreams was to allow us to remain asleep, undisturbed. In an effort to protect the psyche from emotional upset during sleep, a process that Freud termed *displacement* took place. To illustrate this concept, suppose, for example, that you are angry with your mother for dying and leaving you to care for your father who suffers from Alzheimer's disease. Freud would say that your anger at your mother would be hidden in the subtext of the dream. Your emotions would be *displaced* as a way of protecting you from the strong emotions of a more literal dream of, say, shouting at your mother for abandoning you and your father. You might instead dream of your frustration with your dog's slipping out the front door. In this case, your strong feeling of anger at your mother is displaced (with a less intense feeling of frustration) onto your escaping dog as a gentler replacement for your departed mother. This example of displacement is part of a larger aspect of what Freud termed *dreamwork*.

Other Aspects of Dreamwork

In addition to displacement, there is *symbolism*, which occurs when an object, idea, or feeling in a dream is expressed symbolically. As we've already mentioned, Freud often attached sexual meaning to dreams. For example, Freud wrote that a room in a dream generally symbolizes a woman; therefore entering a room may be an expression of sexual intercourse. He was also well-known for his description of phallic symbolism, as in this description from *The Interpretation of Dreams*: "All sharp and elongated objects, sticks, tree-trunks, umbrellas, weapons, knives, daggers and pikes, represent the male member" (p. 371). So, for instance, a dream of a thick tree trunk would indicate potent male sexuality. Freud also coined the term *condensation* to refer to the process in dreams by which issues or emotions are combined. For example, if you dream that your clean-shaven ex-husband has a beard like your father, the image of the ex-husband is condensed with the father. The dream interpretation would rely on your free associations to both your ex-husband and your father.

Finally, Freud noted that dreams can actually be *projections* of our repressed desires onto others. For instance, a woman might dream about her best friend leaving town, when, in reality, it is the *dreamer* who is consumed with wanderlust.

Although Freud is certainly considered a pioneer in the field of dream theory and practice, it was his junior colleague, C. G. Jung, who expanded dream interpretation to deeper layers of the psyche with broader individual applications. And although we respect the many contributions of Freud and others, our particular perspective is informed primarily by the practices and theories of C. G. Jung.

C. G. JUNG

Jung departed from Freud in that he did not focus his view of dreams on disguised sexual wish fulfillment. And whereas Freud was interested in finding the *cause* of a certain dream, Jung emphasized the goal or *purpose* of the dream. Jung, therefore, was interested in *the effect of the dream on the life of the dreamer*. Unlike Freud, who felt that dreams concealed deep urges or wishes, Jung felt that dreams pointed beyond wish fulfillments; indeed, he held the practical view that dreams could help us deal with our current problems.

Two Views of Dreamwork

Jung provides a useful comparison of the two views (Freudian and Jungian) in his analysis of his depressed patient's dream, in Volume Three of *The Collected Works of C. G. Jung*. The dream is simple: "A certain man gave [the dreamer] a peculiar old sword. . . . The dreamer enjoyed this gift immensely" (p. 183). The patient himself interpreted the dream from a Freudian standpoint: he wished for the phallic power of his father (sword) in order to conquer life in a sexual way.

Unfortunately, the interpretation was uninspiring, and the patient remained depressed and fearful. Then Jung tried his approach of amplification by asking for associations to the sword and to the man who gave the sword. The sword represented a "guard against the dangers of life," and the swordsman was his friend, who faced "the dangers of life through brave decision" (p. 184). Jung and his patient agreed that the purpose of this dream was to provide the dreamer with a new attitude of brave decision and power. Jung's patient recovered from his depression and proceeded to live his life with a more hopeful and self-fulfilling perspective. Jung stressed how the influence of this dream expanded the life of the dreamer, a process Jung termed *individuation*.

Individuation is the continual process of realizing one's potential as a unique human being. Jung emphasized (as in the just-cited sword dream) that the meaning of a dream will always contribute to an individual's lifelong development. This *prospective* or forward-seeking understanding of dreams in relation to adult development is a central guiding principle of Jungian theory and practice.

The Personal and Collective Unconscious

Jung thought of the human mind in terms of the *ego*, the *personal unconscious*, and the *collective unconscious*. The ego is a person's sense of identity. Negative self-traits take another form, which Jung called the *shadow*. The personal unconscious (or what Freud called the unconscious) is a place of deep thoughts, feelings, and urges, not directly accessible to consciousness, except primarily through dreams.

Whereas the personal unconscious is shaped by our own experiences, the collective unconscious is that part of the human mind that is—in a sense—inherited. It is our common link to other humans throughout history. Jung studied dreams as well as the hallucinations of his patients and concluded that some images could not have resulted from personal experience (for example, a Texas cattle rancher who dreams of Egyptian hieroglyphics). Jung argued that the source of certain images could not be personal, so the source must be ancestral or *collective*. He explained the collective unconscious as "the deposit of ancestral experiences from untold millions of years," which reflected the deepest experiences of mankind (*The Collected Works of C. G. Jung*, Volume Eight, p. 376).

Archetypes

Jung elaborated the concept of the collective unconscious by developing the idea of *archetypes*. Archetypes are the structural elements of the collective unconscious, and they are represented by images. The word archetype comes from the Greek *arche* meaning "first," and *type* meaning "imprint or pattern." According to Jung, archetypes reflect the shared experiences of all humanity and can be found not only in myths, legends, and sacred literature but also in our dreams.

Jung found that dreams often contained universal archetypal images. By understanding the archetypal image in a particular dream, he was better able to understand the dream. An example is the myth of the hero. The hero is an individual who embarks on a journey to find something that will better humanity. The hero is powerful, resilient, and courageous; overcomes obstacles; and is adventurous. Describing these attributes is an example of *amplification*, a process of gathering meaning to honor what the dream states. The term *honor* is specifically chosen to convey the enhanced effect of the amplified dream on the dreamer.

For example, a sad girl, dominated by an insensitive stepmother, dreams of shoes. She might remember the Cinderella fairy tale and hope for a promising future while searching for a wise older woman (godmother) to guide her. Or a teenage boy who is being bullied in gym class has a dream that reminds him of the biblical story of David and Goliath. By identifying with David, the boy could think of a strategy that would empower him in gym class. These are simple illustrations of how archetypal motifs can be sources of vitality and insight for dreamers.

OUR APPROACH

Although we've briefly outlined the basic dream theories of Freud and Jung, we must confess an affinity for Jung's approach, mostly because it makes good sense for grief dreams by allowing for the individual tailoring of meaning for the dreamer. Although our approach is more selectively Jungian, we will honor our commitment (see the Preface and Chapter Three) to refrain from the use of confusing psychological jargon when possible. For those dreamers in search of a more in-depth psychological analysis, please refer to the Reader Resources section at the end of this book.

THE HEALING POWER OF DREAMS

Death is traumatic, and death requires survivors to grieve. Grief, we discover, is hard work. When we grieve, we soldier ourselves to march through days unlike all our previous days: we exist cocooned in stuffed-cotton shock, bearing the disorientation and pain while we hope to gather memory and meaning. Dreams offer a way through pain to memory and meaning.

The Importance of Sleep

From ancient healers to modern psychologists, the healing power of dreams has long been recognized. Current sleep research confirms this powerful effect. We spend one-third of our day and fully one-third of our lives asleep. And while we sleep, we dream. Most dreams occur shortly after we fall asleep and near morning. Among other things, sleep provides rest and recovery from trauma. While we sleep, we digest our daily experiences. While we grieve, we may have dreams of the deceased. As we've mentioned already in the Introduction, these grief dreams often feature unusual images, special messages, or even nightmares to help us digest the traumatic effects of death.

Dreaming for Memory and Creative Thinking

Sleep research demonstrates helpful functions beyond rest and nourishment: sleep promotes memory and creative thinking. When we grieve, we gather our memories of our lost loved ones as treasures; sleep enables us to have our memories. Sleep experts have demonstrated that memory is consolidated during sleep through complex neurochemical processes, as if a photographic image were developing and gradually creating a permanent imprint during the night. Psychologists emphasize that when we hold memory, we begin to make meaning.

And meaning is our bridge into the future. While we're grieving, the future may seem impossible or out of reach; however, each night while we sleep, we recover our creative capacity to make meaningful futures. In fact, recent research indicates that sleep stimulates creative thinking. So when helpful family and friends tell mourners to "get some rest" or "try to sleep," we know this to be wise counsel for recovery, for memory, and for creating meaning in our lives.

Recalling Your Dreams

While we sleep, we dream, although many people do not recall their dreams. Please be assured that you *are* dreaming and your dreams are helping you with your grief work, whether or not you remember your dreams. Jung wrote of the natural healing function of dreams: how in times of "deep distress," dreams provide an "illumination, a revelation, a saving idea" (in *The Collected Works of C. G. Jung*, Volume Five, p. 294). In the time of deepest distress, after the loss of a loved one, dreams *help us*.

Toolbox: Remembering Your Dreams

Although many people do not recall their dreams, there are specific ways to prompt your recall of your grief dreams:

1. Read this book, immersed in the grief dreams of other mourners, to help stimulate your dream recall.

2. Keep a dream journal at your bedside. This can be part of your grief journal, or it can be a separate journal designated just for dreams. (We will usually refer to this journal as a *grief dream journal*.)

3. Upon awakening, allow a few minutes of lingering in the sleep-wake interlude to see if an image comes to mind. Just remember that image. Don't push for a story line. Write down the image in your grief dream journal and then move into your day.

4. During your day, see if the image or dream fragment is repeated or touched on in some way. Note this in your grief dream journal. For example, upon awakening, you may recall a bird in your dream. While showering, you note the bird was a blue jay. Later that day, you see blue jays in your neighbor's tree. Write these associations in your grief dream journal.

5. Gradually, you will quilt together these dream pieces.

HOW DREAMS HELP US
WITH OUR GRIEF WORK

Dreams are as unique as each individual dreamer. It is difficult, therefore, to make generalizations about dreams, particularly during the exquisitely sensitive period of mourning. Nonetheless, during bereavement, grief dreams have shared features that offer help in four specific ways.

Grief Dreams Absorb Shock

In the early days of grief, dreams provide a way for survivors to absorb the shock of death. Often the scene and the circumstances

of the death are repeated and reviewed in dream form to help grievers digest the reality of the death. While awake, mourners are numb,
disoriented, stunned, repeating the words, "I just can't believe it."
But at night, while sleeping, their dreams are offering doses of the
reality of the death that allow for gradual digestion.

For example, three months after the death of her husband,
Mary explained it this way: "Gradually, each morning when I
awake, I'm less confused. I may hate how my life has changed, but
my life and my loss feel more real to me now. I'm not stumbling
around anymore."

In *Mourning and Melancholia*, Freud termed this process of acceptance of the loss of the beloved as *grief work*. All who mourn know
this work. What mourners may not know is that they are engaged
in this work while they sleep. Sleep offers dreaming experiences that
ease the initial shock of death for all who grieve.

Nightmares are common during early grief, particularly with sudden or unexpected deaths. These dreams terrify us with traumatic
details, often replaying the sad and sometimes frightening circumstances of our loved one's death. Even though nightmares can be
disturbing and frightening, it is important to know that nightmares
are a useful part of the grief process.

Nightmares absorb the shock of unexpected death and help survivors digest the reality of their experiences. For example, in the
weeks following the death of her baby from Sudden Infant Death
Syndrome (SIDS), Patricia was plagued by horrible dreams: "I kept
dreaming, night after night, of when I found my baby, dead. In the
dreams, I hold her, the ambulance comes, I can't stop crying. I got so
turned around that I didn't want to go to sleep anymore—I was
afraid of having that nightmare. But after about a month, I went to
a counselor, and the bad dreams stopped. I'm having more peaceful
dreams about my baby now. Looking back, I think the nightmares
were making me deal with the truth I didn't want to see." We see
from Patricia's story that when we look back over our dreams, particularly our nightmares, our reflections help us in our grief work.

An important tool for nightmare relief is your grief dream journal. Record your nightmares in your journal. Your grief dream journal can provide a protective *dreamcatcher* effect. Dreamcatchers are nets crafted by Native American healers that are suspended above the dreamer's bed to "catch" bad dreams. In the same way, placed beside your bed, your grief dream journal can catch the nightmare you record. Keeping track of your nightmares in a journal will help you remember to review them later for new perspectives. We will give more specific guidelines for tracking and reviewing your nightmares in the Toolboxes in Chapter Six.

Although nightmares are not unusual during bereavement, it is important to remember that if your nightmares are preventing restful sleep, you should consider seeking professional help. Patricia explained how her nightmares stopped after she started seeing a grief counselor. During the counseling, she began to have more peaceful dreams and restful sleep. A grief counselor can serve as a dreamcatcher, listening to the nightmares and offering specific perspectives that are comforting. In addition, a medical evaluation may be necessary for severe sleep disruption. (See Chapter Six for help in nightmare relief and Chapter Nine for seeking professional help.)

Grief Dreams Sort Out Our Emotions

A second shared feature of grief dreaming involves the emotions of the survivor. Intense feelings about the deceased are exposed in survivors' dreams. These emotions may include pleasure, passion, regret, delight, disappointment, joy, guilt, remorse, loneliness, admiration, anger, indifference, relief, anguish, and always, upon awakening, the hollowing sink of loss. "Sometimes, when I first wake up after dreaming about Kevin," says Felicia, "I forget for a few seconds that he's gone. But then, the shock of it all comes rushing back, and I wish that I could return to the dream, to the place where Kevin is alive and grief doesn't exist."

Grief dreams sort out the mourner's emotions and offer helpful images to hold these intense feelings about the deceased. Images such as shouldering a backpack, carrying a basket of kittens, stirring a soup pot, cradling an infant, hugging a shaggy dog, or gathering a handful of wildflowers are examples of how dream symbols give us many new ways to handle our complicated grief emotions.

Miriam describes this emotional process: "I hadn't realized all the feelings I had for my father after he died. At first, I felt so sad and so lost without his strong presence. Then I felt furious that he had abandoned me and upset my life. Then I felt free to live my life more fully. My dreams brought out these feelings, and I began to sort them out. I feel lighter now."

Toolbox: Sorting Out Your Emotions

The following are some simple steps to help you sort through your emotions. We will use this basic framework throughout this book, so it's important for you to begin to work with your grief dream journal. Your journal will become an important tool in your dreamwork.

1. In your grief dream journal, review your dream and <u>underline the emotions</u>.

2. Sort out which emotions you had during the dream and which emotions came after you were awake. For example, you may feel <u>peaceful</u> to see your loved one in your dream and <u>angry</u> when you awake.

3. As you go through your day, note when you feel <u>peaceful</u> and when you feel <u>angry</u>. Write down the situations when these feelings occur. For example, you may feel <u>peaceful</u> when you feed your baby and <u>angry</u> when you have to pay bills. Record these emotional situations in your dream journal. Accept these feelings, without judgment, as part of your grieving process.

4. Over time, this method of sorting out your emotions will help you accept your feelings. You will notice a subtle positive change in your behavior—for example, you may be more patient. Or you may be able to listen more attentively to others. You will be able to accomplish more in your day. By recognizing and sorting out grief emotions through dreamwork, your healing progresses.

Grief Dreams Continue Our Inner Relationship with the Deceased

A third common aspect of grief dreams is that they help the survivor forge an internalized relationship with the deceased. In the following pages, you will read stories of mourners who explain how their dreams gave them experiences with their lost loved ones. In fact, survivors often feel that they have *found* their *lost* loves in an *internalized* way through their dreams. At this point, dreamers welcome their dreams: "I hope I have another dream about my son tonight." "I can't wait to see our baby again in my dreams." "I awake each day thinking of our baby as our guardian angel." "My sister is with me in spirit."

Over time, the deceased may appear older or animated in new ways. "My son was dressed in a college graduation gown." "My newborn is now a toddler in my dreams." These dreams emphasize how grief work has created room to grow. Many mourners experience their dreams as a way to continue their relationship with the deceased and to let it grow with time.

In situations where the grieved relationship had been troubled or complicated, dreams can help the survivor resolve problems. Dreams can be a window for a better understanding of the deceased and may provide a way for explanations and apologies. Often survivors report that their dreams eased their guilt and soothed a more troubled previous relationship.

"I never realized that my father cared about me until this dream where he is comforting me." "My daughter laughed and held my hand—I know the anger between us is gone now." The relationship with the deceased is unknotted and internalized with positive adjustment. Remarkable changes in relationships can occur *after* death through dreams. The following pages offer poignant testimony to this powerful effect of grief dreams.

> **Toolbox: Your Internal Relationship with the Deceased**
>
> What follows are the basics for you to begin to visualize an internal relationship with your deceased loved one.
>
> 1. In your grief dream journal, review a dream where your loved one appears.
>
> 2. Find a detail of the dream that lets you hold on to the dream. For example, if your loved one is standing on a rocky shore, keep a pebble in your pocket to keep the dream with you.
>
> 3. By holding on to the dream, particularly by using an actual symbolic object, you can create space for the internal relationship to grow.

Grief Dreams Make a Creative Bridge to Our Future

In a fourth dimension, as time begins to heal raw grief, a unique aspect of grief dreams unfolds. This is the creative, life-affirming contribution of dreams.

Grief dreams bring insight to the dreamer. A sense of purpose and meaning develops. This meaning-making aspect of grief work (part of what we call denouement) heralds creative self-renewal. At this point, dreamers will say, "*Now* I understand what my dreams are telling me." This inner confidence gives the survivor outer purpose. Investment in the future returns. "I know Mom loves me and wishes me well." "Now I can enjoy my grandchildren, knowing my husband's spirit lives on in them."

The bereaved begins to move forward in life in positive, expansive ways. They treasure dream images that are inspiring for the future. "In my dream, my mother is opening a door to a room in our home I never knew about before." "My sister appears in my dreams, healthy and whole, free of the addictions that ended her life prematurely." These grief dreams are bridges that hold the relationship with the deceased while reaching into new life for the survivor.

As discussed in Chapter One, one of the ways in which we begin to heal from our loss is to find meaning in it. Grief dreams often serve as a springboard for a future action plan that is explicitly named in memory of the deceased. For example, the survivor may organize a charitable foundation, dedicate a work of art, or set a personal goal. These activities serve to channel the energy reclaimed through grief work for renewed living. "I want to live my life worthy of my mother's memory." "I feel I can move on with my life because I know my baby will always be part of me and of our family." Grief dreams anchor our inner relationships and provide a bridge into our creative future.

Toolbox: Grief Dreams as Creative Bridges to the Future

What follows are some helpful suggestions that will enable you to use your dreams as a means of building a creative bridge to the future. In early grief, envisioning the future may seem inconceivable to you. This is normal. Remember that this particular aspect of dreamwork normally occurs as the denouement phase of grief. So if you're having difficulty envisioning building a creative bridge to the future, set this section aside and return to it at a later date.

1. Review the dreams you have recorded so far in your grief dream journal.

2. Look for a symbol of the future: an image that suggests new life. This may be a sunrise or the color green or a flower blooming or a door opening or a young child or animal.

3. Consider how this symbol is meant especially for you and your future.

Now let us turn to actual dreams to illustrate how, in our times of deepest distress, dreams help us. We will begin with the most fundamental of grief dreams, the visitation dream, where we are given the dream-gift of "just one more visit."

3

The Visitation Dream

Thou . . . dost visit oft my midnight dream;
Thy glory meets me with the earliest beam
Of light, which tells that Morning is awake.
                                                William Wordsworth

M y mother visits me regularly in my dreams," says Betty. "It's
always so comforting to just see her again. She never really
says anything, but I don't mind. I'm just happy she visits me every
now and then."

Like Betty, most mourners experience a great deal of consolation in the dreams they have of their deceased loved ones. And, of
the four major types of grief dreams, the *visitation dream* is perhaps the
most uplifting and certainly the most frequent type of grief dream.

TREASURED GIFTS

Visitation dreams are often brief and uncomplicated, which makes
this particular type of dream the ideal starting point for our exploration into the various types of grief dreams. In visitation dreams,
the dreamer usually just spends time with the deceased; there are
no prophetic messages or warnings associated with these dreams.

"I had a dream about my sister, Sherri, about a month after her
death," says Traci. "In the dream, it was just the two of us, doing a

lot of nothing. We were shooting the breeze like we always did and just content to be with each other." Traci's dream accurately captures the essence of the visitation dream: calming, consoling, and *normal*.

Linda's visitation dreams emphasize the consoling nature of this dream type. "It's always so nice when he visits me in my dreams," says Linda of her father's visitations. "Right after he died, it was almost as if he was giving me a little break from grieving for him." Linda's visitation dreams offer her a respite from the intensity of mourning, which she perceives as a gift from her father. For a brief moment, there is no death, no loss, and no grief. Linda feels only the relaxed peace of being reunited with her father.

Visitation dreams come in many forms. Sometimes the dreamer catches only a glimpse of the deceased; other times, the visit is more detailed, perhaps even containing a gentle conversation.

Recurrent Visitations

Most visitation dreams are simple, one-time visits; but sometimes the dreamer reports recurrent dreams that are similar in form and content. For example, Katherine (whom you first met in the Introduction and will meet again in the following section) often has the same dream of her grandfather, usually around the same time of year. He appears in the same hometown bar, near the Thanksgiving holiday.

Recurrent visitation dreams can also evolve and change over time, perhaps reflecting the changing ebb and flow of grief itself. For example, Linda's dreams of her father were once vivid and detailed, but over time, her father has become less of a central character. "Most of the time in the dream, I know he's there," says Linda, "but he rarely speaks and is not usually the focus of the dream in the way he was right after his death."

Linda feels that her father's gradual fading into the background of her dreams reflects the diminished intensity of her grief. That is, soon after her loss, when the pain of grief was more acute, her father assumed a more dominant role in her dreams. "It was almost as if he was trying to just sit with me and comfort me," she says of her earlier visitation dreams. After several years, Linda says, "I still miss him, but I'm accustomed to life without him now. Maybe that's why he is no longer center stage in my dreams."

Recovered Memories

A visitation dream may also recover some (usually forgotten) memory of the dreamer, often from childhood. For example, you may dream of your deceased mother, but the "setting" of the dream is in your childhood home, not your New York City apartment. Your mother may appear in the dream as she did twenty years ago, perhaps in some memorable event, such as a Christmas party. Or you may capture a specific detail from your dream that evokes a memory, such as dreaming of your uncle in his signature blue vest, the one he always wore at family gatherings.

How to Read the Dream Sequences

All of the dream stories presented in this book will follow a similar format, designed with the needs of grieving people in mind. We know that in grief, mourners often experience an inability to concentrate and absorb new information. So we've tried to refrain from using complicated psychological jargon and long explanations for what we believe to be simple self-help steps. We have instead carefully outlined each dream sequence and have framed the self-help steps in the Toolbox for easy reference. Remember, too, that we maintain the position that the *dreamer* is in the best position to determine the meaning of the dreams. The self-help tips, then, are merely suggestions that may allow for further dream exploration and understanding.

The format of each dream sequence is quite simple. In the following visitation dreams, we'll first read about the dream and the feelings the dreamer had upon waking. Then we'll learn more about the dreamer and his or her relationship with the deceased through the back story. All of this information is then woven together to *amplify* or make meaning out of the dream. Finally, because understanding how each dream is helpful to the dreamer and—more important—how each dream story can help *you*, the Toolbox rounds out each dream sequence.

We begin with Katherine's dream of her grandfather, an uplifting, comforting visit that brings a granddaughter much peace.

KATHERINE'S DREAM: GRANDPA'S VISIT

The surroundings seem gloomy and nondescript, almost like being in a hometown bar. It is quiet. I am in this place alone, when I turn and see that Grandpa is with me. He is dressed in work clothes. We smoke together. Neither of us speaks, but we look each other in the eyes and communicate without words. Then he is gone.

Feelings upon Waking

When I wake up, I feel loved, comforted, and protected. The feeling lasts a long time, and just recalling the dream can reinvigorate those feelings.

The Back Story

My grandfather had fifteen grandchildren and I'm the oldest. I was fourteen when he passed away after suffering a heart attack. In the years before he died, my grandparents moved down south because of Grandpa's health. My uncle purchased their home when they moved away. The last time I saw my grandfather was in March when my family made the drive down because Grandpa was in the hospital. He passed away in May and we had a memorial service for him. He was cremated. I remember crying at the service and feeling weak because my dad and brother weren't crying at all. I felt in my heart that Grandpa was in heaven, but I cried because I would no longer be able to see this strong man sit and read the paper, drink coffee, laugh, or play with his grandchildren.

Sometime later, my mother and I visited my uncle who was living in my grandparents' old house. In one of the unused bedrooms upstairs, we saw the urn that had held my grandfather's ashes. The urn reminded me of a tobacco canister, one of the fancy ones my dad used to have.

When Grandpa's ashes were scattered, it was an "adults only" event, but even as an adult, I've never visited the place where his ashes were scattered. I feel guilty about this, but as time passes, I feel as if it's too late. I remember hearing that Grandpa wanted to be cremated because he didn't want people going to a cemetery and crying over a concrete marker. To me, this meant that being cremated and having his ashes scattered was a way for him to be free to be with us.

Comments

Katherine's back story offers clues to help us understand the meaning of her visitation dream. First, the setting of the dream, a quiet hometown bar, sets the tone of the dream and reflects the quiet way the two communicate throughout the rest of the dream. Her grandfather's attire, casual work clothing, contributes to the relaxed atmosphere of the dream.

Katherine and her grandfather do not speak to each other in the dream but communicate through eye contact and in sharing a smoke together. Both ways of communicating are intimate and loving; no words are necessary for this pair.

As Shakespeare observed, the eyes are the mirror of the soul. Although dreaming of the eyes (or eye contact) can mean many things, in Katherine's dream, the eye-to-eye communication is clearly symbolic of the soulful connection she has with her beloved Grandpa. The sharing of a smoke, too, affirms this soulful connection. The two sit, like old buddies in a bar, inhaling each other's smoke.

The smoking connection in Katherine's dream and the mention of her grandfather's cremation are striking. Shortly after her grandfather's death, Katherine tells us that she sees the urn that held his ashes and is reminded of her father's tobacco canister. Katherine voices regret because she was not included in the ash-scattering ceremony and guilt because she has not yet visited this sacred place. In Katherine's dream, her grandfather returns to share a smoke with her, almost as if to assuage her feelings of regret and guilt regarding his earthly remains. Because of her grandfather's visit, the urn that resembles a tobacco canister—once the focus of her guilt and regret—can now be viewed positively, as the dreamer makes new connections between the tobacco canister (urn, ashes) and smoking with her grandfather.

Katherine has had the same visitation dream many times since her grandfather's death ten years ago. "I often have this visitation dream of Grandpa around Thanksgiving," she says. As families gather around the table and celebrate their many joys and blessings, Katherine receives a special blessing from her beloved grandfather. "I feel that he visits me to remind me that he is still with me, protecting me, watching me, and loving me."

How Katherine's Dream Helps Her

Katherine's recurrent dream helps her grieve in the four specific ways outlined in Chapter Two:

1. She digests and adjusts to the reality of her grandfather's death.

2. She sorts through her feelings, including guilt.

3. She develops an internal relationship with her grandfather: "He is still with me."

4. She makes a bridge from past to present to future each Thanksgiving.

Toolbox: How Katherine's Dream Can Help You

You can create a similar experience for yourself by using your own visitation dream. If you have not yet had a visitation dream, the following suggestions will work by simply recalling a pleasant memory of your loved one. For example, you might recall a special time you spent with your loved one, such as a holiday gathering or a quiet walk in the park. Whenever you feel the need to revisit the comforting sense of your deceased loved one, try following the simple steps outlined here. Close your eyes (or concentrate) and recall a positive dream or memory of your loved one.

1. Imagine that you are at this moment back in the dream or memory. Notice carefully the scene. Outdoors? Indoors? Time of day? Quality of the light? Weather? What do your senses tell you? What do you smell? What do you hear? What do you touch? What do you see? What do you taste? Allow yourself to be fully present in the scene of the dream or memory.

2. Pay attention to any images or symbols in the dream. For example, Katherine is able to make a connection between smoking—the tobacco canister and her grandfather's urn—and her unresolved guilt over not visiting the place where his ashes were scattered. If you are having trouble understanding the images and symbols in your dream, note these symbols in your grief dream journal and then consult a dream dictionary to help give you some idea of their meaning. (*The Complete Dream Book* by Gillian Holloway is a good choice. See, also, the Reader Resources section for other ideas.)

3. Concentrate on the effect that the dream or memory has on you. Are you consoled? Relieved? Delighted? At peace? Pay

attention to the specific elements in the dream or memory that led to these feelings ("My father hugged me" or "My dog ran up to me and licked my face"). The goal here is to learn to conjure these healing images so that you can revisit them over and over again, as needed. Katherine notes that just recalling the images in her dream brings about a feeling of peace. The primary goal of this exercise is to help you tap into your own healing dream images so that you, too, can experience a sense of peace during this difficult time.

The close and loving relationship between Katherine and Grandpa is affirmed in this lovely visitation dream. This comfortable, easy connection is a common element in visitation dreams and is likewise an aspect in the following dream that Frank describes about his mother.

FRANK'S DREAM: A VISIT FROM MOM

Someone in the dream pointed to my mother—and there she was, at a distance. She turned toward me and smiled as she walked closer. In the dream, I was quite conscious of the fact that she was dead, but there she was, so I figured I might as well go along with it. We talked briefly, not about anything special, but it was warm and cordial and suffused with a kind of good humor that convinced me at the end, things were OK with her. And then it was over.

Feelings upon Waking

I awoke with a smile and a deep sense of peace.

The Back Story

I had this dream about a year after my mother's death, while planning the Jewish custom of dedicating her gravestone. My mother died in 1997, and I was already in my early fifties. Mom died at age eighty-five, full of years and service. For the last fifteen years of her life, she enjoyed doing volunteer work at a home for the blind.

In the years since my mother's death, I've had the chance to see our relationship more clearly than I ever really allowed myself when she was alive. Sometimes I'm very angry at the things she said and did back then. Like my father (who died ten years earlier), she had no qualms about the use of physical violence. While I may have had serious reservations about some of her child-rearing techniques, I must say that in our later years we had evolved into good friends.

We had the ability to spend quality time together, laughing at similar things, each able to appreciate the ironies and absurdities of existence, and each able to (more or less) overlook what each may have seen as the other's shortcomings. Most important, we pretty much had said everything—good and bad—that needed to be said to one another.

Comments

The cordial, relaxed relationship that Frank shares with his mother is the focus of this visitation dream. This relationship contrasts sharply with the fearful, traumatic relationship Frank had with his father (see Chapter Six). In this way, the dream separates the parents, accenting the positive relationship Frank has with his mother while keeping his father out of the picture completely.

In the dream, someone alerts Frank to his mother's presence, and he catches sight of her from a distance. The dream plot brings her into focus. She is first "pointed out" from afar and then draws closer. It is Frank's mother who turns toward *him*. She smiles, and she approaches him. Frank senses that his mother is dead, but he makes a decision to just go along with things. (As we shall see, it's fairly common in grief dreams for the dreamer to know that the loved one is indeed deceased and to likewise make the decision not to mention this fact.) Mother and son have a brief conversation that is filled with good humor. This warm conversation leaves Frank with a feeling of well-being regarding his mother.

Frank's visitation dream has a good-humored tenor that mirrors the relationship he shared with his mother in their later years together. In the dream, Frank sees his mother from a distance, but he does not approach her. It is his mother who takes the initiative to move closer to her son, and in so doing, she is brought into focus. In Frank's back story, he admits that his mother was not always the best parent. He expresses anger and hurt over some of the things his mother did and said to him when he was a child. This might explain his reticence to approach her in the dream.

Frank's mother has no such qualms. The moment she sees him, she smiles and moves toward him. Initially, Frank is suspicious. After all, his mother is deceased. But he soon relaxes and decides to go with the flow. In the same way, at some point in Frank's life, he made the decision to forgive his mother for some of her questionable child-rearing practices. As a result, Frank and his mother became closer—friends, even. And toward the end of her life, the two enjoyed a relaxed and caring relationship. Not only were mother and son able to speak openly about a variety of topics, but their conversations, like the dream exchange, were infused with good humor and laughter. There is no rancor or confrontation, for the two have evolved beyond the hurt of the past; they are able to overlook each other's shortcomings.

Finally, the pleasant exchange between the two yields a special gift for the dreamer: Frank feels a sense of peace at the end of the dream because he knows that all is well with his mother. The confidence expressed by the dreamer regarding his mother's well-being indicates the dreamer's personal growth as reflected in his back story.

How Frank's Dream Helps Him

Frank's dream helps him grieve in three specific ways:

1. He is adjusting to the reality of his mother's death.

2. He is sorting through his emotions.

3. He is having an internalized relationship with his mother that grows with time.

Toolbox: How Frank's Dream Can Help You

Frank's dream ends when he awakes with a smile. A reaction, such as a smile, can be used as a memory prompt to recall the peaceful effect of the dream. In other words, by repeating the act of smiling, Frank can bring back his peaceful experience of his mother. Try this with one of your dreams:

1. Select a visitation dream where you have a distinct reaction. This can be a reaction you have in the dream or upon awakening.

2. Now, concentrate on the dream and repeat your reaction—smile, laugh, nod, sigh, exclaim, gaze upward—whatever your reaction was, repeat it now.

3. As you repeat your reaction, let it prompt your emotional memory of the dream. Fully feel the effect of the dream.

4. Inhale slowly, letting the dream inspire you by breathing it in. Exhale and feel refreshed.

5. Write this memory prompt in your grief dream journal for future assistance.

Frank, like Katherine, is comforted by his visitation dream. Both dreamers report feelings of peace and love upon waking. And both dreamers are able to receive and internalize the positive feelings that come from their visitation dreams.

But often, the healing aspects of grief dreams are not as immediate. Sometimes it takes time and reflection before the meaningful aspects of the dream can emerge. In the following visitation dream, the dreamer is unable to initially discern these aspects. Over time, however, she gains a great deal of consolation and meaning from her visitation dream.

JANET'S DREAM:
MY MOTHER'S RED SWEATER

I am in bed, taking a nap at my parents' home. I hear my mother's voice; she's trying to wake me. I sit up in bed and see her bustling around. She is telling me to get ready, that my father wants us to go to the hospital now. She is young looking and vigorous. She is wearing her bright red sweater. I am aware that she wants us to go and attend to her on her deathbed. It seems as if she is mainly concerned about doing what is proper and in fulfilling my father's expectations.

Feelings upon Waking

I woke from this dream feeling devastated. The contrast between my mother's healthy vitality in the dream and her true condition is almost too much to bear. I cry for a while before I am able to pull myself together.

The Back Story

I had this dream a couple of weeks before my mother's death. She was in the hospital, in the end stages of leukemia. I had come from out of town to be with my mother and was staying in my parents' house. My brother had flown in from California, and along with our father, the three of us were making frequent trips to the hospital to be with Mom. This particular dream occurred after one such visit, when I had returned to my parents' house for a nap.

My mother's actions in the dream were very much in character. She was a vital person, who liked things to flow smoothly. She always wanted everyone to be happy and cooperative. I can easily imagine her rounding up the three of us for a trip to the hospital!

She died what I would call a "good death." Her death was rela-
tively uncomplicated and she was not too uncomfortable. She was
well cared for and surrounded by loved ones. She was eighty-three
and had suffered from acute leukemia for about a year. She was
ready to go, and the family was relieved that her ordeal was over.

Mom was a gentle and very creative person, an artist, who led a
rather sheltered and constricted life. I generally felt thoroughly loved
by her, especially as an adult, but I rarely felt understood. I gradually came to accept this as just the way things were. At the time of
her death, I felt reasonably comfortable with our relationship.
Although I wasn't aware of any particular loose ends left dangling—
that is, any that we would have been able to realistically discuss and
resolve—I somehow had a sense of a backlog of love left over that
I had not gotten around to expressing. I think my grief was greater
because of this.

Comments

Janet's dream of her dying mother illustrates how the grief process
often begins before the actual death of someone we love. Janet's
mother, we are told, is in the final stages of leukemia. Her daughter
has already begun to mourn her passing, as illustrated by this dream.

Janet's mother is the central figure in the dream, full of energy
and vitality. She assumes a maternal role in the dream, reflective of
her role as mother in life. In this role, she busily herds together her
family for a journey, just as she had probably done in life on countless occasions. Janet's mother, like most homemakers of her generation, is concerned with doing the right or proper thing and living
up to her husband's expectations.

It's not surprising that the setting of this dream is in Janet's
childhood home (a common setting in grief dreams). Not only is
she staying in her parents' home as she attends to her dying mother,
but the dream about her mother takes place on her mother's "turf"
as a homemaker. As discussed previously, it's fairly common in

visitation dreams (and in dreams in general) to recover memories. The childhood home setting sets the stage for the memories that follow. In the dream, her mother resumes her important role as mother and homemaker, a role age and illness have taken from her. In this role, Janet's mother appears young, healthy, and active—just as Janet remembers her from childhood. Janet's mother is a veritable whirlwind, bustling around in her bright red sweater, attending to the tasks at hand. Red, the color of vitality, energy, and passion, further enhances the image of a mother who is very much filled with life and vigor.

In contrast to this vivacious image of her mother, her mother's actions, as Janet describes them, are centered on pleasing her husband and doing what is proper. Janet tells us in her back story that even though her mother was a creative, artistic, and vital person, like many women of her generation, she led a life that was somewhat sheltered and limited. Perhaps the contrasting images of a dynamic and energetic woman who is also bound by her duties as wife and mother are reflected in Janet's visitation dream.

Janet initially finds the dream to be a painful reminder of her mother's impending death. She feels "devastated" upon waking from a dream of a healthy, vital mother to the stark reality of a dying one. This sad paradox gives this dream a certain poignancy. Despite Janet's initial sadness, however, she will come to view this dream positively.

"I think the dream was helpful because after I had the chance to process it," she says, "I had the sense that regardless of my mother's physical situation, her spirit was still vital and eternal."

How Janet's Dream Helps Her

Janet's dream helps her in two central ways:

1. Her dream enables her to adjust to the devastating reality of her mother's impending death.

2. Her dream helps her internalize her mother's spirit as "vital and eternal."

Toolbox: How Janet's Dream Can Help You

The red sweater worn by Janet's mother is the vibrant feature of this dream. By wearing a red sweater, Janet could feel connected to her mother's vitality and vigor. In this way, Janet can actually wear the dream image as a memory prompt. Follow these steps for this type of dream memory prompt:

1. Select a tangible dream image such as clothing or an object that stands out in your dream.

2. Make this image visible in your everyday life: wear, carry, or display it.

3. You will feel the positive effect of the dreamwork on you as you keep the dream specifically with you.

4. Record the effects in your grief dream journal. Reviewing your dreams will bring the message home.

Janet's visitation dream is helpful in our exploration of grief dreams because it illustrates that quite often we're unable to crack the nut of our own dreams until we're ready to receive the message. This is why it's so important to keep a record of your dreams so that you can turn them over in your mind and review them at a later date. Once Janet moved from the disbelief and disarray phases of intense grief, she was able to finally grasp the healing message of this beautiful dream.

In the following dream, Alison, like Janet, is able to grasp the meaning of her dream only after she had spent many years processing her sister's death. Alison's dream also reminds us that grief is not confined to a predetermined timetable but is indeed the work of a lifetime.

ALISON'S DREAM: ROSSIE'S SHOWER

The dream took place in the house where I now live. My house is surrounded by national forest, and there is a breezeway that is partially open to the elements. Rossie came down from the attic and walked out into the breezeway, to a portion that extends out beyond the roof and into the open. There, she was going to stand on the stone flooring, out in the open, and take a shower with rainwater. I witness her movements and actions, but I was not engaged with Rossie at all in the dream.

Feelings upon Waking

My feelings upon waking were not profound, but I did feel a sense of freedom and self-differentiation—the kind that can come from acute clarity.

The Back Story

My sister Rossie committed suicide. For many years, I have had a lingering sense of guilt about Rossie's death. I felt guilty for not having been able to prevent her death and even, at times, guilt around my own existence. Lately, some of my idealized notions of Rossie have begun to be tempered with the reality of her own weaknesses and the awareness that maybe—just maybe—I am not responsible for her death. As this has happened, I have begun to feel less guilty.

It has been many years since I have had a dream of Rossie. This particular dream came twenty-seven years after Rossie died and seems to give expression to an internal process that is taking shape. In the dream, Rossie comes down out of my attic, where she has been out of sight but present in my house. She comes out into the open, separate from the house, and is exposed for a shower. In a sense, she is "coming clean," and as she does, I, too, come clean.

I think this dream symbolizes and affirms something that is happening in my grief process. Despite the many years since her death, on a conscious level, I have continued to remain tangled in my own feelings of guilt and responsibility. Now, a separation is taking place: Rossie has come down out of the attic and left my house and is about to "come clean." This sense of separation, of letting her be responsible for herself and her own actions, underscores my emerging sense of interior freedom and differentiation.

Comments

Alison's own impressive analysis of this dream helps clarify its meaning. In the dream, Rossie comes down from the attic and goes out into the light of day to take a rain shower. Alison is a detached, unengaged observer in the dream.

Alison first mentions that Rossie emerges from her attic, a place in dreams where old thoughts and feelings are stored as keepsakes but are not used. In Alison's case, these old thoughts include her feelings of guilt and responsibility for Rossie's death as well as her denial of her sister's weakness. These old thoughts and feelings need to be aired out and brought into the light of day. Rossie is the harbinger of this action.

She comes out of the attic and into the open sunlight to shower. Alison notes that Rossie is "exposed" and out in "the open"—just as Alison's dusty old thoughts and feelings of denial are now opened up and exposed. Rossie is intent on taking a rain shower. Rain, often a cleansing image in dreams, can also bring forth new life; it comes from the sky, evoking images of heaven and spiritual growth.

Alison is merely an observer in the dream; she is not engaged in Rossie's actions or movements but watches from a distance. The disengagement from her sister's actions reflects Alison's dawning sense that she is not responsible for Rossie's decision to take her own life. This is a milestone in Alison's grief journey.

How Alison's Dream Helps Her

Alison's "coming clean" dream separates her from the traumatic past of her sister's suicide and demonstrates the ongoing nature of bereavement. Alison's dream also helps her in three important ways:

1. Now, twenty-seven years later, Alison feels more detached from Rossie's life; she's no longer "tangled" in feelings of guilt and responsibility.

2. Alison's hopeful future of "interior freedom" is affirmed by the dream.

3. Her dream provides a bridge from the past to the present to the future.

Toolbox: How Alison's Dream Can Help You

Over time, dreams can bring new perspectives. Like Alison, our dreams can help us all "come clean." In order to experience the healing benefits of a dream like Alison's, you can actually *enact* the dream by using a featured action in the dream as a memory prompt. Here's how it works:

1. Select a dream with a clear action involved. For example, in Alison's dream, a rain shower is the central action that prompts Alison to reflect upon the cleansing aspects of the dream.

2. Repeat the dream action to harness the power of the dream. Alison might let the rain drench her or might simply take a shower. If your visitation dream features, say, a canoe trip or a barefoot walk through the cool grass, you could simply reenact these features of the dream. Your intentional reenactment will engage the powerful effect of the dream.

3. Remember to breathe to *let in* the full experience.

4. Record the experience in your grief dream journal for future reference.

Visitation dreams are almost always peaceful, soothing, and comforting. Indeed most mourners awake from these dreams feeling uplifted and consoled. But beyond the solace we gain from our visitation dreams is the opportunity they offer us for healing. Of course, we recognize that some mourners may not yet be ready to engage the steps outlined in the Toolboxes. But just knowing that there are healing actions available to you when you *are* ready can be a great comfort.

As we move from the simplicity and beauty of visitation dreams to the more overt nature of message dreams, we hope that you take with you the tranquility and peace that are the hallmarks of the visitation dream.

The Message Dream

*I think very few of those who have lost their beloved
have failed to receive some sign or message from
them in dreams, and often it is of deep and abiding
consolation.*

William Dean Howells

M y mother was the sort of person who liked to tell everyone what to do," says Shauna. "She was the queen of unsolicited advice. On more than one occasion, she has come to me in a dream to give me advice about relationships (which I'm not very good at). She usually just says her piece and then vanishes."

Shauna seems certain that her mother is actually communicating with her through dreams, but is this really possible? Before we move forward in our exploration of message dreams, let's step back and address this question.

TWO VIEWS

Most people seem to ascribe to one of two views. One view holds that Shauna's dream is nothing more than the fulfillment of her own desire to have her mother back again. Those of this view would probably regard Shauna's dream as a product of her unconscious, manufactured as a way of helping her to cope with her loss. This is not to say that those of this view fail to recognize the vital role dreams play in helping us to work through the complex emotions of grief, only that some may hold reservations about embracing the idea that the deceased have the capability to somehow enter our dreams.

The second view would disagree with this analysis and assert that it is indeed possible for the deceased to communicate with us through our dreams. This view is certainly reflected in most of the world's great religions, and it is a position held by many of the bereaved persons who contributed to this book. Although this view may or may not be grounded in a particular religious tradition, most who express this view tend to believe in the concept of a soul and an afterlife. (See Chapter Eight for more on grief and faith.)

In truth, there is much we don't know about sleep and dreams; so our position (briefly stated in the Preface) is one of openness. Because we do not ascribe to one view over the other, we have chosen to present all of the dreams in this book from the perspective of the dreamer. Regardless of the perspective, however, our focus remains on the effect the dream has on the dreamer.

COMMUNICATION FROM
THE DREAMSCAPE

Message dreams usually impart advice, information, instruction, or even warnings from the deceased. Messages can be conveyed in an overt manner: "My husband came to me in a dream and told me to have the chimney swept in the fall." Or they can be conveyed through the use of symbols: "My baby held on to a white balloon and floated upward, giggling."

Messages can be uplifting, funny, consoling, or hopeful; conversely, though less often, messages can be confusing, frightening, disturbing, or bizarre. Most dreamers, regardless of the message, prefer to view message dreams positively.

A Different Language

Dream language is usually quite different from waking language. Because symbols constitute the language of dreams, our task is to "learn the lingo" so that we can decipher the meaning of our dreams. Usually, certain symbols or images appear in the dream, and if we don't speak the language, we may miss the message.

"For three nights in a row, my daughter appeared in my dreams, sitting on her bed, reading a book," says Edna. "In the dream, I stood in the doorway and watched her. It was clear that she was reading to me, but I couldn't hear what she was reading and I couldn't see the title of the book."

Edna expresses some initial frustration in relating this dream; that is, until she finally understood the language of her dream. "A few nights after the third and final book-reading dream," says Edna, "I felt compelled to go into Amber's room. I looked in the drawer of her nightstand and then under the bed. As I held on to the side of the bed to steady myself, I noticed a small book wedged between the mattress and the box spring. The book turned out to be Amber's journal. Her journal helped to explain the pain she was feeling shortly before she took her life. Although it was difficult to read, I felt comforted by the loving way she wrote about me and her father and sister. I think she wanted me to find the journal so that I would know that she did not die because of us."

Another key aspect of Edna's dreams of Amber is that in the dream, Amber speaks, but Edna is unable to hear her. This is a very common feature in grief dreams, particularly in message dreams. In both Susan's and Cory's dreams in the following sections, the inability to hear the deceased is a source of anxiety and even fear for the dreamer. Sometimes the deceased will speak from behind a wall or window; other times, they will speak too softly to be heard or in a different language, which the dreamer does not understand. When this happens, other symbols in the dream usually help convey the message. The image of Amber on her bed, reading a book, turned out to be a sufficient means of conveying her message.

Proxy Messages

A proxy message dream contains a message delivered to the dreamer that may be intended for someone else. For example, Nancy's husband appeared in a dream and delivered a message for their son: "Tell Timmy that I'm proud of him for making Eagle Scout." Nancy's proxy message was quite clear, but sometimes the dreamer does not understand the proxy message at all. It is only after the message is shared with someone else (usually the intended recipient of the message) that the meaning is apparent.

"I dreamed that my friend Ana was brushing her long dark hair and smiling," says Sondra. "I really didn't understand the meaning of this dream until I shared it with Ana's husband, Gary. He told me he recently gathered together Ana's cosmetics and put them into a box to throw away. He was unable to part with her hairbrush, however, because it still had strands of Ana's hair in it. He keeps the brush on his dresser and sometimes 'talks' to it." Both Sondra and Gary felt that Ana was sending a message to Gary through Sondra and that she was somehow pleased that Gary had decided to keep Ana's brush.

Finally, some proxy message dreams are a combination of both direct and indirect messages. These *dual message dreams* usually contain an obvious message for the dreamer but also a message for someone else that may or may not be understood by the dreamer. (See Ellen's dream later in the chapter.)

Reading the Message Dream

As you read through the following message dreams, try to discern the elements discussed previously. Learning how message dreams work is the key to unlocking the messages in your own dreams. Indeed some messages may not at first be recognized by the dreamer and might be missed. But even if you think you may have missed a message, it will likely come around again in another dream. Dreams often give us many chances to hear our messages.

SUSAN'S DREAM: JACKIE'S SIGN

I dreamed there were bees in my youngest daughter, Bethany's, bedroom, causing her to scream and run away. I ran into her room and quickly swatted the bees out the window. Looking to tell her that her room was now free of bees, I went out the back door of the house in which I had grown up. My father and brother, Russ, were out in the yard. Dad was sitting on our old, red picnic table, the one he had made so many years ago. Russ was rinsing out the small, colorful, fish-themed plastic wading pool my children played in when they were toddlers. Neither had seen Bethany, so I called out for her.

At that moment, I felt someone come up behind me and press against me. Then that someone wrapped their arms around me tightly and with much care. Wondering who it might be, Jackie's face came full around to look me straight in the eye. She was smiling, and the glow that radiated about her exuded love. My spirit was immediately lifted beyond words. My Jackie was there!

She was quietly mouthing words I couldn't understand. Needing so badly to hear her message, I asked her to repeat her words, all the while knowing full well that she had passed away many years ago. Even though she repeated her message, I still could not hear. Her words were soft and muffled, so once again, I asked her to repeat what she said. At this point, she gently took my hand in hers and began doing what I suspect was sign language, in the palm of my hand. Her hands felt warm, soft, and smooth, just like they always were.

By this time, I was beginning to panic, worried I would never know her message and she would disappear. I felt such urgency to tell her, "I love you! I miss you!" Her hand grew still, she stopped signing, and then her smile grew wide. Her face came closer. So close, it touched my cheek. All the while, I could still feel the length of her body pressed against mine. Sadly, the dream slowly faded, and she was gone.

Feelings upon Waking

I awoke and found myself lying on my side with my arms wrapped around myself, sobbing. The feel of Jackie, her physical presence, was still very much with me, and I refused to move for fear that I would lose the *feel* of Jackie. I lay there, silent, eyes closed, for several minutes, reveling in the sweet caress of my lost daughter. As my tears subsided, a comfort washed over me.

The Back Story

During the summer of 2000, I was beside myself with mixed, bittersweet emotions—emotions so powerful, I finally sought the help of a therapist. Therapy I so badly needed and never received after the loss of two of my four daughters.

My first loss came at the hands of the narrow-minded thinking of the 1960s when, as an unmarried, pregnant, seventeen-year-old, I was forced to give up my firstborn daughter, Joanne, for adoption.

My second loss happened in 1990 with the death of my sixteen-year-old daughter, Jackie, from leukemia. I'm certain that the reason for the sudden surge of emotions was that my third-born daughter, Kristine, was getting married that week, and although I was happy and excited for her, I felt devastated that Jackie would not be there. Even though I was filled with delight because I had reconnected with my daughter Joanne in 1999 (and she was going to serve as a bridesmaid in Kristine's wedding), I worried about how I would survive the day without Jackie.

But this dream made me feel as if Jackie had entered my soul to soothe the ten-year wound that resulted from her death. And I think she wanted to remind me that she *is* always with me. It's been nearly four years since this particular dream occurred, and there are still times when I can actually feel her body's warmth at my back, or by my side. I can still envision her beautiful, bluish-green eyes peering into mine.

I will always cherish the love we shared.

Comments

Like Janet's dream (in Chapter Three), the setting of this dream is in Susan's childhood home. Susan's dream begins with her swatting bees from her youngest daughter's bedroom. When these industrious insects appear in dreams, they usually represent work ("busy as a bee"), unless, of course, the dreamer has a specific story or association with bees (for example, a bee allergy). Bees work to protect the queen; they clean and service the hive and produce honey. The "hum" of busy bees no doubt reflects the flurry of activity taking place in Susan's life as she plans for her daughter's wedding.

A deeper meaning may point to the ongoing hum of grief work that has been so much a part of Susan's life. Bees, like grief work, can be troublesome, relentless, and intrusive. And like the sting of a bee, the "sting" of grief is painful and long lasting. Grief intrudes even during moments of great happiness and can sting us when we least expect it. In the dream, Susan assumes her role as mother and protector, clearing her frightened daughter's room of the bees that have terrified the child. But unlike the bees in Bethany's room, grief cannot be swatted away; it buzzes around the impending wedding, demanding attention.

The picnic table from the past is a symbol for family recreation. Susan mentions that the table is red, a color we recall from Janet's visitation dream (Chapter Three) as a symbol of life and vitality. In the same way, weddings, in general, are life-affirming events and occasions for families to gather and celebrate alongside the happy couple.

The child's swimming pool in the dream probably symbolizes the dreamer's personal unconscious situation (pools or bodies of water in dreams usually symbolize the unconscious). Susan's psychic energy and her current situation are essentially "pooled" and contained. Her memories of loss—the baby, Joanne, whom she gave up for adoption so many years ago, and the daughter, Jackie, whom she lost to leukemia—remain fixed or pooled in her unconscious. As she prepares for her daughter's wedding, the grief hovers alongside the happy activities, whispering an obvious reminder: someone is missing.

All of these symbols seem almost a prelude to Jackie's surprising appearance. Jackie comes from out of nowhere and embraces her mother from behind. Susan feels the familiar weight of Jackie's body as it presses against her own. This intimate gesture reaffirms the eternal bond between mother and daughter. Jackie's playful smile and radiant appearance lift Susan's spirit and fill her with great joy.

Jackie's visit brings with it a message—a message that Susan is eager to understand—but Jackie speaks too softly for Susan to hear. Susan, like many other dreamers (see Cory's dream and Julie's dream later in the chapter), experiences anxiety about the dream message. Because the language of dream messages differs so greatly from day-time messages, dreamers, like Susan, may be at first caught off guard, frightened, or anxious because they are unable to grasp the message being conveyed in the dream. Emotionally, in the dream and upon awakening, the dreamer may initially experience this language difference with panic and incomprehension. As Susan puts it, "She was mouthing words I couldn't understand. . . . I still could not hear. . . . I was beginning to panic, worried I would never know her message and she would disappear. I felt such urgency."

Jackie, however, seems unperturbed by Susan's inability to receive the message and merely resorts to an alternative method of communication: she begins signing her message into Susan's palm. Jackie's signing into Susan's palm in the dream is an effective symbol, conveying Jackie's hands as they "always were" and also "handing" Susan a message about how she will "handle" the upcoming wedding without Jackie. Dreams often give us double-entendres and puns to help us "get it." Coupled with Jackie's overall playfulness in the dream, it seems likely that this is Jackie's way of helping Susan to "get the message."

Perhaps the most striking aspect of this message dream, however, is in the physical contact between mother and daughter. Susan physically feels Jackie's presence, first in the surprise embrace that heralded Jackie's arrival, and then in the continued pressing of her daughter's body against her own as Jackie works to convey her message. The hand signing is also an intimate, loving, physical action. Jackie's farewell, signaled by her moving closer to her mother and gently brushing her cheek against Susan's face, is perhaps the most powerful and enduring moment in this dream. It is so powerful, in fact, that Susan feels the lingering physical sensation of her daughter upon waking (this sort of lingering physical sensation that survives the dream is common in grief dreams). The moments after waking are sacred to Susan, and she lies still in her bed, reveling in the aftereffects of this treasured reunion with her daughter.

How Susan's Dream Helps Her

In the denouement phase of grief, dreams can continue to aid the dreamer in the ongoing adjustment to the reality of loss. Susan eloquently describes how through this dream Jackie entered her soul to "soothe the ten-year wound" inflicted at the time of Jackie's death. The impending marriage of her daughter Kristine highlights Jackie's absence in a new and painful way. Susan's dream of Jackie helps her better deal with this new surge of grief in the following ways:

1. Susan continues to sort through her feelings of sadness and love for her cherished daughter.

2. Susan is reunited with Jackie in a real and tangible way. Susan "feels" the physical presence of her daughter, affirming Jackie's continued presence in Susan's life.

3. The dream offers a bridge from past to present to future. At the time of the dream, Susan was at a crossroads, concerned about how she would survive the upcoming wedding without her third daughter. The initial images of the red picnic table and plastic pool are from the *past*, when the girls were little, and Jackie was alive. Jackie's felt presence is in the *present*. The immediate *future* problem of the wedding is solved by Jackie's presence.

Indeed Jackie's message to Susan is clear: Susan will have *all four* of her daughters at the wedding.

Toolbox: How Susan's Dream Can Help You

As life marches on without our loved one, we often wonder how we'll cope with holidays, birthdays, weddings, and the various other family celebrations. How can we celebrate when our joy is obscured by the harsh reality of death? The overwhelming feeling that someone is missing—and indeed, that person *is* missing—can deepen the pain of grief at a time when we're supposed to be happy. It is often during such times that our loved one will appear in a dream to offer, or "hand us," messages of courage and comfort. Let us now examine the aspects of Susan's dream that can also be helpful to you.

1. Jung wrote, "Often the hands know how to solve a riddle with which the intellect has wrestled in vain" (*The Collected Works of C. G. Jung,* Volume Eight, p. 86). With this insight in mind, search your own dreams for hand imagery. For example, have you recorded dreams of your loved one waving, beckoning, or holding your hand? If so, make note of these dreams and review past dreams for messages you may have missed initially.

2. Consider what your hands mean to you. They enable you to touch, feel, make contact, gesture, and pray. More metaphorically, your hands give you the capacity to "handle" your situation.

3. The situation that mourners are often handed comes in the form of the inevitable holidays and family celebrations that are part of life. Such occasions are often dreaded or seem irrelevant; the idea that life goes on without your loved one seems impossible and can intensify grief. A grief dream, how-

ever, can offer a new perspective that can help you handle your feelings during these occasions. The following are some specific tips to help you better cope with triggering events:

- Focus on the holiday that you are particularly concerned about.

- Plan ahead. Know that your grief will be intensified during this time.

- Decide on a life-affirming activity that both honors your feelings and memorializes your loved one. For example, you might decide to plant a rose bush on the one-year anniversary of your mother's death or release twenty-one red balloons on your son's birthday.

- Watch for a dream. Often, in planning such activities, a dream will emerge to show you how to handle this holiday.

4. Remember to write, in your own *hand*writing, your insights about how you are holding your feelings, how you are making contact with your loved one, and how you are handling your life and the impending holiday at this moment.

Susan's message from Jackie fills her with joy and gives her courage to face the busy and chaotic days before Kristine's wedding. In the following message dream, the message conveyed from Chris to Cory, like Jackie's message to Susan, is initially baffling. Chris, like Jackie, finds an alternative method for conveying his message that points to the sometimes overt nature of message dreams.

CORY'S DREAM: A MESSAGE FROM CHRIS

In the dream, the phone rang in the middle of the night, and I picked up the receiver in the kitchen. I knew that someone was on the other side,

*yet I couldn't hear who it was. I guessed it was Chris but couldn't be sure.
I began to feel afraid. I listened intently but realized that I was wearing
earplugs, which may have prevented me from hearing Chris's message.
Even after I removed the earplugs, however, I still couldn't hear Chris.
Then, the line went dead, or I hung up, I can't remember. I went back
into my bedroom, and standing next to the bed was a large, outdoor mailbox. I was incredibly startled by the sight because I knew that Chris had
somehow managed to place it there. I couldn't understand how he had the
power to move something so large from the street to my bedroom. I began
to yell and woke myself up.*

Feelings upon Waking

I woke up feeling very startled, disturbed, and on the verge of tears.
It was a very real and intense dream.

The Back Story

Last summer, on the way back from a weekend trip with my wife, I
received the shocking news that my older brother, Chris, had died
in a kayaking accident. He was thirty-five. Suddenly, my little
brother and I were without our crazy big brother. Chris lived very
intensely and not without struggle. He had problems with drinking
and it was in his nature to live dangerously. The night he died, he
was out kayaking alone after dark without a life jacket. For me, I felt
some anger that he couldn't seem to pull his life together and drop
the dependence that began during his adolescence. But I knew it
wasn't up to me, even though I often wished I had the power to
change things.

Chris was an aspiring filmmaker and his company was aptly
named Rogue Scholars Production, a name that fit him perfectly.
Though he was often stuck at that perpetual bratty twelve-year-old
stage, he was still one of the smartest people I knew. He was well
read, almost to a ridiculous degree, and he was a creative, original
writer.

Overall, as adults, my brothers and I shared a good relationship. Chris had a great sense of humor, which in truth, sometimes made me squirm, and he took some delight in that. But without a doubt, I know he loved us. Even though Chris is gone, I still feel close to him and in some ways even closer than before, as he is never out of my thoughts. I love him very much.

After I wrote about this particular dream in my dream journal, I realized that the dream contained a direct message from Chris to me. When Chris was alive, our primary means of communication was the telephone (we lived far from each other). In the dream, I tried to hear him on the phone but couldn't. Maybe this aspect of the dream pointed to the fact that we can no longer talk on the phone. But what did the mailbox beside my bed mean? This stumped me for a while, but then it hit me: I think Chris was telling me that from now on we would have to communicate through dreams.

Comments

Cory's dream begins with a late-night phone call, which he answers not at his bedside, but in the kitchen. Telephone calls are common in grief dreams, and dreamers, like Cory, are usually frustrated because they are often unable to actually speak with the deceased. The first part of Cory's dream illustrates this anxiety. (Cory doesn't know for certain if it is Chris calling, but he suspects that the caller is indeed his brother.)

Cory might be tempted to think that the phone call is simply one of Chris's jokes, but Cory is not amused; in fact, he tells us, "I began to feel afraid." Cory's initial fear is a common reaction in dreams of this type. The prospect of actually establishing contact with the deceased often stirs fear, anxiety, and sometimes excited anticipation. Cory thinks the earplugs he's wearing prevent him from receiving Chris's message, but even after the plugs are removed, he is still unable to hear his brother. He eventually returns to his bedroom, where the second part of the dream unfolds.

Cory is shocked to find an outdoor mailbox by his bed. He marvels at the strength involved in moving such a large structure, and he knows intuitively that his brother is responsible. Chris, it seems, will go to great lengths to maintain contact with Cory. Cory describes Chris as a bit of a prankster, so it seems fitting that Chris should convey his message in this unorthodox way. Cory's reaction to the mailbox resonates with the way in which Cory often reacted to Chris's jokes. Cory is initially confused and startled (he squirms) and wakes from the dream yelling.

Chris delivers a powerful message of filial devotion, but, like Susan, Cory takes a while to "get it." Later, as Cory reflects upon his dream, he reaches a startling conclusion: communication between the two brothers is still possible though the dreamscape and, of course, through Cory's conscious imagination. Once Cory understands Chris's message, he feels comforted by it.

How Cory's Dream Helps Him

Part of Cory's grief work is to mourn the absence of telephone communication with his brother, which Cory describes as their primary means of interaction. Although it's true that Cory can no longer talk to his brother on the telephone, the mailbox message from Chris presents another option: communication through his mind and via dreams. Cory's dream helps him in the following ways:

1. He continues to adjust to the reality of his brother's death: "We can no longer talk on the phone."

2. He sorts through his emotions: "I began to feel afraid"; "I woke up feeling very startled, disturbed, and on the verge of tears"; "It was a very real and intense dream." (It is important to remember that dream contact with the deceased can cause fear and anxiety as well as anticipation.)

3. He develops an internalized relationship with Chris in the dreamscape.

Toolbox: How Cory's Dream Can Help You

Cory's message dream is an example of the power of dream symbols. The sudden appearance of the mailbox in the dream is so shocking that Cory ponders the dream until he catches the message. The following are some suggestions to help you catch the message of your grief dreams:

1. Begin by reviewing your grief dream journal for symbols of communication: telephones, letters, books, computers, people talking, physical features of mouths, eyes, ears. Underline these symbols of communication. Focus on one communication symbol, and think about how this symbol may point to a new way of communicating with your loved one. For example, if your communication symbol was a letter, you might consider writing a letter to your loved one. If your communication symbol was a book, find a book important to the deceased that you could read to feel close to your loved one. Of course, at any moment, you can reconnect with your loved one by simply calling his or her image to mind. Many mourners find great comfort in maintaining an ongoing dialogue with their loved one while jogging, driving to work, or just before falling asleep at night.

2. Think about the communication symbol as a way to help you reach out in your grief work by communicating with people alive in your world right now. We know that human contact is important for mourners. Your dream may be a message from your deceased loved one reminding you to communicate with important people in your life for comfort and support. For example, Cory could also understand the mailbox by his bed as a message from his deceased older brother, Chris, to keep in close touch with their younger brother in order to share their

> mutual loss. Or if you have written a letter to your loved one as suggested in step one, you might now take the next step of reading the letter aloud to a family member or to your grief partner as a way of reaching out for support. Remember that each dream communication symbol will give you a key to accessing more support for yourself by contacting people in your life in various ways—by telephone, by letter, by e-mail, or by sharing dreams in conversation.
>
> 3. Write your communication messages in your journal as reminders to reach out for support and comfort.

Both Susan and Cory receive messages that are clearly intended for *them*. These messages address a particular situation or certain issue (Susan's daughter's wedding, Cory's new way of communicating). Sometimes, however, message dreams contain messages that are intended for someone other than the dreamer (a proxy message dream). The dreamer may not understand the message until the dream is shared with the person for whom the message was intended. In the following dream, the dreamer receives two messages: one for the dreamer and the other for the dreamer's mother.

ELLEN'S DREAM: A GRANDMOTHER'S MESSAGE FOR TWO

One week before my mother was scheduled to undergo some rather invasive medical testing, I had a message dream about my grandmother Edith. In the dream, I was in a black room. Gazing to the far end of the room, I spied my grandmother walking toward me with a small green bird bouncing back and forth around her head. I could hear her saying, "No, Petey, no!" This continued until she was about three feet away from me. She stood still and the bird stopped bouncing. My grandmother looked right at me and said in a calm voice, "Your mother will be OK." Then, with one swift, smooth move, she turned around and walked away. The small bird resumed his bouncing around her head, and she continued to tell him, "No, Petey, no!"

Feelings upon Waking

I felt thrilled to have seen my grandmother again, and I felt a sense of comfort from her message. The peace and hope of the dream stayed with me for days.

The Back Story

My grandmother Edith and I had been very close. I loved her almost more than life itself. She was a very active woman; she loved to walk and swim. As she grew older, it became more difficult for her to do these activities because she suffered from Alzheimer's disease. The disease progressed slowly, but eventually, she was placed into a nursing home. This was devastating for both my mother and me, but I was only nineteen at the time and couldn't do much about it. I did visit her often, though. My grandmother passed away in her sleep in February 1994.

Several months after her death, she began visiting me in my dreams. This particular dream occurred around the time my mother had been experiencing some problems with the arteries in the left side of her neck. She was scheduled to have an angioplasty about a week after this dream. When I drove my mother to the hospital for the procedure, I told her about the dream. She listened and then looked away, unable to speak for about five minutes. When she composed herself, she told me that when she was a little girl, she actually had a green parakeet named Petey and that the bird would often fly around both my grandfather's and grandmother's heads. My mother recalled my grandmother shouting at the bird, "No, Petey, no!" I was astounded. I had never heard about the bird before this dream.

Interestingly, when we arrived at the hospital, we were told that my mother would not need an angioplasty after all. The blood work revealed that the new medication my mother had been taking apparently resolved the problem. So we went shopping instead!

Comments

We first met Ellen briefly in the Introduction as she shared a reassurance dream about her friend Paula. The first thing we might notice about Ellen's dream of her grandmother is the contrast in colors. Like the dream Ellen had of Paula, the dream of her grandmother begins with Ellen in a black room. Black is the absence of all colors; the death of her grandmother brought Ellen an "absence," and given the potential risk of her mother's angioplasty, the dream suggests Ellen's underlying concern for more absence.

As in Frank's dream of his mother (Chapter Three), Ellen's grandmother (as well as the small, green bird) is spied at a distance and then moves closer to her. We later learn from Ellen's mother that Petey was, in fact, green. But also, his green color in the dream stands in stark contrast to the black room. Green is the color of spring vegetation and new life, and birds often represent deep thoughts or spirituality. The bouncing green bird and Edith's animated admonishments draw attention both to the deliverer of the message and the message itself.

Ellen's grandmother, now clearly in focus and standing only a few feet away from the dreamer, is ready to deliver her message. Notice how the bird stops bouncing when Edith delivers the message, almost as if the bird, too, recognizes the importance of the message. Once the message is delivered, Petey resumes his bouncing and Edith exits the dream.

As it turns out, Ellen's grandmother has a message not only for Ellen but also for Ellen's mother. This twofold message makes this a very rare and special type of message dream. The message Edith gives to Ellen is direct and to the point ("Your mother will be OK"), whereas the message intended for Ellen's mother is less direct. In fact, Edith's second message—conveyed through the image of the small, green bird—is not immediately clear to Ellen. The image of Petey fluttering around her grandmother's head is so striking, however, that Ellen is sure to remember it.

When Ellen reveals the dream to her mother, her mother is speechless. Of course, Ellen's mother immediately recognizes Petey, and after a few moments, she shares the childhood connections with her daughter. The message for Ellen's mother is a powerful one: as Ellen's mother faces the possibility of an angioplasty, she receives the much needed support of her own mother, Edith. The vehicle for delivering this message is through her daughter, Ellen.

This lively, hopeful, and animated message dream gives both mother and daughter courage and comfort as they face a potentially invasive medical procedure. Edith wants both women to know that they are not alone during this challenging and uncertain time.

How Ellen's Dream Helps Her

Aside from delivering a message from her grandmother to her mother, Ellen's vivid message dream helps her in several important ways.

1. Ellen's dream helps her as she continues to digest the reality of her grandmother's death and comforts her as she faces the reality of her mother's impending medical procedure.

2. She sorts through her feelings (sad, happy, amazed, and—though unstated—worried about her mother's condition).

3. Ellen continues to develop an internal relationship with her grandmother. Edith not only visits Ellen regularly but also gives messages both to Ellen and her mother.

4. Ellen makes a bridge from the past (her mother's childhood and her own), to the present (preparing for her mother's procedure), to the future ("Your mother will be OK").

Toolbox: How Ellen's Dream Can Help You

As we have already seen in this chapter, dreams that may not have initially been understood by the dreamer often make a great deal of sense later on. This is one reason why keeping a grief dream journal is so beneficial. What follows are some specific instructions that you may find helpful in deciphering your message dreams:

1. If you have been keeping a grief dream journal, take some time to review your dreams specifically for messages you may have overlooked.

2. Once you've located a particular message dream, spend some time reading and rereading the dream to determine how the message might be meaningful to you or—as in Ellen's case—to someone else.

3. Be aware that many message dreams contain more than one message. For example, in Ellen's dream, the first message was literally a verbal message: "Your mother will be OK." The second message was implied in the image of the parakeet, Petey, a message that only Ellen's mother would fully understand.

4. Once you have determined your message, write it down. In Ellen's dream, she might write the following:

My grandmother's appearance with the parakeet is striking to me: I'll ask Mom about that. Perhaps she can understand why my grandmother is talking so familiarly with a green parakeet named Petey.

5. Writing down your messages will help in two ways:

It will remind you to talk to people in your life who might be able to clarify the meaning and share the message with you in a comforting, supportive way.

Ellen's dual message dream is an excellent example of a message dream as well as a proxy message dream. Her dream demonstrates that message dreams can come in many different forms. As mentioned in Chapter Two, not all grief dreams fit into just one category. For example, Cory's dream has elements of both a trauma dream and a message dream. Although speaking of grief dreams in terms of genre or category can be helpful, it's important not to become too fixated on a particular category, because you run the risk of missing something important within the dream. The following dream may at first appear to be a reassurance dream, but after reading both the dream and the back story carefully, you'll see that it's clear that this is indeed a very special message dream.

JULIE'S DREAM: A HEAVENLY CONCERT

One morning, over thirteen years after my brother died, I awoke slowly from a very special dream. In the dream, my parents and I were watching my brother, Bill, conduct a symphony orchestra concert. Bill was standing up high on a stage several feet away from us. He was wearing some type of a dark coat that looked similar to a graduation robe. As we watched Bill on the stage, I felt a sense of anxiety and panic since I knew that he was dead. I was worried that my parents wanted to leave, so I told them that we had to stay for the entire performance. In fact, I kept insisting that we stay together until the end because I knew that Bill had only so much time. We watched Bill as the music played. He looked as strong and tall on the stage as he had looked in life. He seemed happy and about the same age as he was when he died. I felt so happy to be in his presence and so glad that my parents were there, too.

Feelings upon Waking

I slowly awoke with the feeling that Bill was still conducting the music. In that blurred state between sleep and wakefulness, I tried to cling to the dream, hoping that time would stand still. When I was fully awake, I felt comforted by the memory of being with my brother. This feeling was very strong and stayed with me through-out the day. I was eager to call my parents and share the dream with them.

The Back Story

My younger brother and only sibling died suddenly at the age of twenty-six from a brain aneurysm. The last time I saw him was on my wedding day, just a month earlier. His death was devastating for both my parents and me.

Bill was a science writer, working as an editor for a technical magazine in Manhattan. He had a degree in journalism and in-dustrial engineering. I always admired how Bill was able to combine his interests and talents in his career and still have time to pursue his first love and great passion, music. Ever since he was young, music had been a big part of Bill's life. Whether he was playing the piano or composing songs, Bill was happiest when surrounded by music.

One of my favorite images of Bill, captured in a treasured photo, occurred on a hot summer afternoon when his band was playing at a local festival. As my parents and I walked downhill and ap-proached the festival, I tried to catch a glimpse of Bill on the stage. The keyboard player was tall, like my brother, but wearing a bright, shiny colored robe that was open in the front, unlike anything Bill would ever wear. Or so I thought. As I got closer, I realized that the keyboard player was Bill and he was having such a great time! After awakening from my dream, I thought back to that summer day and how happy I had felt watching Bill on stage.

One of my major regrets was that my mother and I did not get to see Bill's college graduation. On the same day as his graduation, I was receiving my law degree, some three hundred miles away from his college. My mother stayed with me, and my dad went to be with Bill. After my ceremony, my mother and I quickly made the trip across the state to join my dad and brother for a family celebration. We had a great time together, but I remember feeling sorry that I didn't get to see Bill in his graduation robe.

After awakening from my dream. I had the feeling that it was OK that I didn't get to see Bill's college graduation because, in my dream, my parents and I were witness to something more incredible and meaningful. I knew that Bill was continuing what he had begun in his lifetime. He was happy and creating on a whole new and different level.

So much has changed since he died. My children, whom he never met, are growing up fast and becoming more independent. At the time of this dream, I had been feeling like I was at a crossroads in my life. I was asking myself some tough questions. Should I go back to work? What type of job did I really want to do? How would I find a way to balance everything?

During the many years since Bill died, I've had several dreams about him but few as real to me as this one. Although Bill spoke no words in the dream, just seeing him looking happy and in an environment that he loved was wonderful for me. Now, when I think of the dream, I feel happier and hopeful about my own life.

Comments

In examining Julie's dream, several important aspects of the dream emerge. Bill is "high" above his parents and sister, as they watch him "conduct" an orchestra. Julie mentions that Bill wears a "graduation" type of robe, rather than the traditional tux and tails of a conductor. The whole family is present in the dream, and Julie is insistent that they "stay together." She even expresses fear that her parents might leave the concert early.

When Julie reflects upon the dream, she sheds light on the meaning of many of the symbols. Recall that in her back story, Julie tells us that because she was graduating from law school on the same day her brother graduated from college, she was unable to attend his graduation. Julie says she felt a great deal of regret about not being able to see her brother in his "graduation robe." But in her dream, she is given the chance to finally see him in his robe. Bill is the center of attention and Julie is in the audience, just as she would have been had she attended the graduation. This, of course, is the "graduation of all graduations" in that it seems to symbolize Bill's graduation into a new stage of his existence (notice that Julie names her dream A Heavenly Concert).

Julie also writes about her family's decision to split up so that each child would have one parent in attendance during the dual graduation ceremonies. Even though this seems like a reasonable alternative in such a situation, it is clear that Julie still regrets that she missed out on an opportunity to see Bill shine. Her concern in the dream about her parents' possible early departure from the concert seems to reflect Julie's regret over splitting the family on Bill's (and Julie's) graduation day.

The graduation robe is also connected to Julie's present situation. She tells us that she is "at a crossroads" in her life and is asking herself some "tough questions" about her own future. She is considering a move from her career as a stay-at-home mother to a career outside the home, but she is uncertain if she'll be able to "balance everything." Hence, the theme of commencement and graduation reflects Julie's current conundrum.

Julie mentions a summer concert she attended when Bill appeared in a shiny long robe that seemed out of character for him. She enjoyed seeing Bill just having a good time with his band and his music. Her dream of his conducting the orchestra stirs pleasant memories of that summer day.

Julie's dream allows her to reconnect with her beloved brother during a turning point in her own life. Her brother appears elevated, often a dream symbol indicating growth or a higher perspective, often in a spiritual way. Bill is several feet away, but still close, indicating that he is still very much a part of Julie's life. In fact, Bill seems to be helping Julie to answer some of those nagging questions and concerns about juggling her many commitments. In the role of conductor, Bill brings together a variety of instruments and creates order and harmony. Perhaps she, too, can harmonize the diverse aspects of her own life into a new creation. So, in many ways, the graduation aspect of this dream resolves Julie's regrets by bringing the family together for a dream graduation as well as empowering her to push past the crossroads in her life in order to imagine new possibilities.

How Julie's Dream Helps Her

Julie's adjustment to her brother's death continues, thirteen years later. Like Alison's dream (in Chapter Three), Julie's dream demonstrates the ongoing adjustment that is part of the grief process. Julie's dream helps her in the following ways:

1. She sorts through her feelings: in the dream she feels "happy to be in his presence" but also a sense of anxiety and panic because she knows Bill is dead (recall Frank's dream of his mother, in Chapter Three). Upon awakening, Julie feels comforted by the memory of being with Bill and is eager to phone her parents to tell them of the dream.

2. She feels a strong internal connection with her brother through her dream, affirming that the sibling bond cannot be severed, even by death. This dream also helps her resolve an old problem; namely, her guilt about not attending her brother's graduation.

3. Julie's dream illustrates the fourth function of grief dreams: building a creative bridge to the future. Julie, who is at a crossroads in her life, reports feeling happier and more hopeful about her future because of the dream.

Toolbox: How Julie's Dream Can Help You

The messages in Julie's dream are not immediately apparent. Like many of the dreams presented thus far, the deeper message of the dream requires Julie to reflect upon the dream and the possible messages it may provide concerning her future. The following suggestions can help you reflect upon messages within your grief dreams:

1. Consider the future-pointing role of grief dreams. As you reread Julie's dream, think about how your own dreams might give you messages about your life and your future.

2. Review your grief dream journal for messages that seem to point to the future. These messages may be obvious—such as your aunt appearing in a dream urging you to take a family vacation—or they may come in the form of a symbol, such as a green traffic light, a wedding dress, a bridge, or a road map for a trip.

3. Think about your present life and what questions you are asking yourself: "Should I take that job?" "What is the best way to help my son?" "Should I make arrangements for a nursing home for my mother?" Consider how your dream messages might help you with these questions.

4. Write these insights about your life into your grief dream journal.

Each of the message dreams presented has unique imagery and a distinctive language. For Susan, the symbol was her daughter mouthing words she couldn't understand, then signing into her palm to convey the message that their contact would not be in words, but in the everlasting *feel* of Jackie's presence. For Cory, the symbol was a mailbox by his bed, symbolizing a transition in communication with Chris, from letters or phone calls to *dream mail*. Ellen's dream message was simple and clear: "Your mother will be OK." The message intended for her mother was also obvious, at least to Ellen's mother, thanks to the dream image of Petey. Finally, for Julie the image of her brother dressed in a graduation gown helps resolve her guilt about missing his graduation and helps her grapple with current questions about her commencement into a life outside the home.

Let's turn now to the dream type whose central purpose is to console: the reassurance dream.

5

The Reassurance Dream

The joys of meeting pay the pangs of absence.
Nicholas Rowe

Reassurance dreams are by far the most complex of the four major types of grief dreams. These particular dreams are distinctive in that they are always dreams of consolation and comfort.

"In my dream," says Patrick, "my father looked young and healthy, the way he looked when I was in high school. He was smiling and loading his golf clubs into the trunk of our old Ford. I felt so relieved to see him looking like his old self. The cancer destroyed so much of his body, I was afraid I'd forget what he looked like before he got sick."

Patrick's dream reassures him that his father is restored, healthy, and looking as he did in Patrick's youth. "When I woke up, I felt really good," he says. "I like to think that Dad is healthy again and playing golf with some of his buddies in heaven."

THE DIFFERENCE BETWEEN MESSAGE DREAMS AND REASSURANCE DREAMS

Although reassurance dreams are quite common during all three phases of grief, sometimes it's difficult to differentiate a reassurance dream from its close cousin, the message dream (see Chapter Four).

Reassurance dreams can and often do contain messages, but they differ from message dreams in several important ways.

First, unlike message dreams, which can contain positive or negative messages, reassurance dreams are always dreams of consolation; their "messages" therefore are always positive and often uplifting. Second, reassurance dreams are always intended for *the dreamer*. Message dreams, in contrast, may contain messages for someone other than the dreamer (proxy messages). Finally, unlike message dreams, which are usually fairly random, a reassurance dream always addresses a particular question or concern of the dreamer. For example, in Patrick's dream (mentioned previously), his father appears healthy and free of the cancer that ravaged his body. Patrick expresses concern that he might forget what his father looked like before the cancer, and the dream seems to directly address this concern.

The Back Story Is Key

Sometimes a dreamer's questions or concerns are obvious in the dream story; but, more often, a careful examination of the back story is necessary in order to distinguish a reassurance dream from a message dream. Notice how the following dream changes from a message dream to a reassurance dream once the back story is added.

Lily's Dream

"I had my dog, Sophie, put to sleep in the morning, and that night I had a dream about her," says Lily. "In the dream, it was a beautiful, sunny, warm day. I was standing in the street when I looked up and saw Sophie running down the street like a puppy, legs flying. She stops, turns, and looks at me. Her eyes are smiling at me. We look into each other's eyes. I know she is all right. She turns and keeps running with her tail wagging. And then, I woke up."

Lily's Back Story

Notice how the back story differentiates this dream from a message dream:

"I was very surprised to see Sophie and overjoyed that she could run again. I knew deep inside that she was happy to have been released from such a tired body. I knew she had to be put to sleep, but I agonized over the decision. My heart ached with the responsibility of having her life in my hands. Once the decision was made, we spent a week indulging Sophie. We took her to the beach (her favorite place) and she ate ice cream. It was a beautiful, but sad time. I believe that Sophie was telling me that it was all right that she died that day. The dream ended any doubt that I carried. I thanked Sophie for the dream and the reassurance that my intuition was right; it was time. My sadness was eased and I felt peaceful."

After reading Lily's back story, it is clear that Lily had doubts about her decision to euthanize Sophie. Lily's reassurance dream, then, functions concretely to address those concerns—to console and reassure her that the decision over which she had agonized was indeed the right decision.

Although Lily's dream lacks any specific references to God, heaven, or any particular religious beliefs, it does have a certain spiritual quality, which is quite typical of reassurance dreams, as in Charles's dream, which follows. (For more on the religious aspects associated with grief dreams, see Chapter Eight.)

Charles's Dream

"I had a dream that Bruce was running in the Boston Marathon," says Charles. "People stood on the sidelines cheering, and he waved at them and smiled as he breezed past. He ran past my old childhood church (which isn't even anywhere near Boston!). My pastor, who had died years ago, was standing on the steps of the church waving to Bruce and giving him the thumbs-up sign. Bruce waved back and smiled. I was watching from the sidelines and I felt so happy. I somehow knew that Bruce was in heaven."

Charles's Back Story

Charles's dream of Bruce seems at first to be a message dream (in which, like Patrick's dream, the message of a restored body is conveyed through the image of a healthy Bruce). It is, however, a clear example of a reassurance dream, but it makes sense as such only after we learn the back story:

"My best friend, Bruce, wasn't always such a good guy," says Charles. "When he was younger, he was really into drugs, which often caused him to make some pretty bad decisions. He even spent a year in jail. In his later years, he pulled his life together and was a hard worker. He died of lupus. He was sick for a couple of years before he passed. I used to worry about him, and I feel bad for even saying this, but I was afraid that maybe God would hold some of his past deeds against him. My dream seemed to be telling me that Bruce was no longer in pain, but healthy and happy. I think the image of the church and my pastor was to let me know that Bruce is with God now. This dream made me feel better about everything."

Charles's dream, like Lily's and Patrick's dreams, addresses a specific question or concern. Charles's question surrounds Bruce's ultimate fate in the afterlife: Would God hold Bruce's past deeds against him? Through the reassuring images in the dream, Charles's question is answered: his friend is indeed with God.

Reading the Reassurance Dream

The differences between message and reassurance dreams are often subtle. The central difference is rooted in the positive manner in which reassurance dreams answer questions or concerns of the dreamer, as opposed to the mixed positive or negative communication of a message dream. In the dreams that follow, try to employ some of the techniques you've learned thus far to decipher the meaning of the dreams. For example, you might consider simply reading the dream, the dreamer's feelings upon waking, and the back story. Then, putting the book aside for a moment, make some notes about your understanding of the dream and its meaning.

Try to identify the dreamer's central question or concern and how the dream attempts to resolve it. Ask yourself this: How is this dream reassuring to the dreamer? How does this dream concretely help console the dreamer? This brief exercise will allow you to practice some of your newfound interpretive skills and at the same time teach you to begin to search for reassurance in your own dreams.

VALERIE'S DREAM:
A BOAT RIDE TO HEAVEN

My grandson, Brian, and I stood on the beach, watching as waves pushed gently toward the shore. It's a beautiful day and we are happy. I noticed that Brian was looking at something in the distance, and when I followed his gaze, I spotted a small boat rowing toward us. Brian was happily waving at the man rowing the boat, as if they were old friends. As the boat moved closer, I recognized my son as the skipper. He looked happy; he was smiling. The little boat approached the beach, and my son signaled for Brian to get into the boat. Brian climbed aboard with much joy. My son looked over at me and smiled, as if to say, "Everything is fine, Mom." Then, he resumed rowing, and I watched as the boat disappeared over the horizon.

Feelings upon Waking

I felt happy and peaceful, feelings I had not felt in a very long time.

The Back Story

In less than two years, I lost my only son and my mother, both to cancer, and my eight-year-old grandson to a rare liver disease. Death was like a tornado, thundering through my life, leaving shattered hopes and broken hearts in its wake. There are no words to describe the anguish of losing so much in such a short period of time.

For grieving people, the nighttime is always much worse than the daylight hours. I don't know what it is about darkness that intensifies grief, but for me, it's always worse at night. I would spend hours trying to sleep, usually succumbing to exhaustion just before dawn, which is when I had this dream. I had been crying before I fell asleep, thinking this night about my two boys—my son and my grandson—and wondering if they were together in heaven. I tried to imagine the two of them together in some far-off place, but my faith had been badly shaken by their deaths, and it was difficult for me to truly believe that they were indeed OK in the world beyond. I *wanted* to believe this, of course, but really, how could I know for sure?

But then, I had this dream, this lovely, comforting dream. I have come to believe that this dream was a gift from my son, a kind, gentle man who cared deeply about others, especially his family. I believe he sent this dream to me to console and reassure me that my loved ones do indeed live on in a place—not so far away—just over the horizon.

Comments

Valerie's sensitive description of nighttime being so difficult for the bereaved has been shared by world cultures throughout the ages. Likewise dreams of boats and the sea are common grief dream themes all over the world. These three aspects—nighttime, boats, and the sea—are also persistent themes found in ancient religious and funereal practices. In many mythologies, the treacherous night is understood as a "sea journey" whereby the sun is carried by boat from sunset to sunrise.

Ancient Egyptians used boats as a means of conveyance of the dead to their next life. In medieval times, slain heroes, such as King Arthur, were carried on boats to the Island of the Blessed. In many preliterate cultures, there is a sacred ritual of sending the deceased out to sea in boats. Many ancient religions referred to the sea as the *great mother*. Valerie's dream, although wholly unique to her particular journey of loss, is profoundly connected to mourners throughout the ages. This connection gives her dream a certain timeless quality.

Valerie's dream, at first, seems to be a double-reassurance dream, which includes both Valerie's son and grandson. Although Valerie also suffered the loss of her mother, she tells us in her back story that on this particular night, she was grieving for "my two boys." (Mourners who have suffered multiple losses in a short period of time tend not to grieve for their loved ones collectively.) But even though Valerie's mother is not an active character in her dream, we can see that her mother is invoked symbolically, behind the scenes, in the images of the sea and in her son's final words. And when Valerie repeats the unspoken words of the dream, "Everything is fine, Mom," she is also invoking her own mother with deep reassurance and comfort.

How Valerie's Dream Helps Her

As Valerie writes, "There are no words to describe the anguish of losing so much in such a short period of time"—son, mother, and grandson. It is unspeakably tragic. Likewise there are no words in this remarkable dream. Instead there is a peaceful beach scene in which the brutal reality of the losses of son and grandson can be absorbed in the image of the two rowing out to sea. The imagined words, "Everything is fine, Mom," also bring reassurance through association to Valerie's mom. More specifically, Valerie's dream helps her in the following ways:

1. Valerie sorts through her feelings: she experiences profound sadness and shaken faith as she falls asleep and then feels comforted and restored by this lovely dream.

2. Through this dream, Valerie gains an internalized image of her son and grandson peacefully together in a setting she can now imagine. "Everything is fine," and Valerie rests peacefully with this inner truth.

Toolbox: How Valerie's Dream Can Help You

Religious faith and spiritual values are often profoundly affected by grief. Quite often, the very faith that we thought would sustain us does not. But as Valerie's dream demonstrates, grief dreams can help us as we grapple with the weighty theological questions so common during bereavement. (See Chapter Eight for more about faith and grief and religious images in grief dreams.)

Valerie's dream is also an example of how we can ask for a dream to help us. Indeed she falls asleep with a question that is answered by a dream; this answer ultimately affirms her faith. What follows is a method for you to use as a possible technique for inducing a reassurance dream of your own. Of course, this method doesn't come with a guarantee: we don't always get the dream we want exactly when we want it. Still, many have tried this method with positive results.

1. Before falling asleep, formulate a simple statement or thoughtful intention that captures what you want or need. For example, "I want to feel more peaceful and less angry about my father's death" or "I want to know my loved one is all right" or "I want to find a way to manage the upcoming holiday." We know from sleep research that sleep stimulates creative thinking and restores memory; in other words, we are working even when we're sleeping. This sleep work also helps us with our grief work.

2. When you awake, write down the dreams you recall. If you don't remember a dream, let your mind relax into a daydream. Write down whatever thoughts and images come to mind, even if they don't initially seem to answer your question. Then reconsider your question and see how the images of your dream or daydream might be helpful. For example, you

may have asked, "How will I get through the day, feeling so sad?" And you awake with the image of a seagull. Imagine how a seagull flies with the air currents; see if you can let your grief be like a seagull, carried by the wind of the day.

3. Repeat this exercise several times during the week and record your results.

RAE-ELLEN'S DREAM: ENCOURAGEMENT FROM LOIS

Just days after my sister's funeral, I dreamed that I walked up an enclosed stairwell into an unfamiliar apartment. When I entered the apartment, I saw Lois, sitting at the breakfast bar. My immediate reaction was surprise, but I was also happy to see her. I said, "Oh, Lowie, why did you have to die?" She said, "I was just so tired. I needed to rest." I felt relieved, but then, I thought of her husband and children. "But what about Russ and the girls?" I asked. She replied, "Don't worry; they'll be all right." She seemed to really know that they would. And then, I woke up.

Feelings upon Waking

My first thought upon waking was that I wished we could have talked longer. I wished I had touched her. Another immediate thought was that my sister was OK and that I, too, would be OK. I also felt comforted by the dream, and I was anxious to share the dream with her husband.

The Back Story

When I shared this dream with Lois's husband, he told me that Lois had been very tired ever since a miscarriage earlier that year.

My sister, Lois (whom we called Lowie when we were children), was just thirty years old when she died suddenly on December 10, 1976. The afternoon before, she and her family had gone out to buy a Christmas tree. When they returned, she complained of an awful headache and went upstairs to bed. Her husband decided to sleep on the couch that night so as not to disturb her. Lois died in her sleep from a cerebral hemorrhage.

Lois and I were only eleven months apart. We played together a lot, although she was a tomboy and I loved my dolls. We shared a bedroom until we were teenagers. Our arguments were generally about borrowing each other's clothes and neatness (or her lack of it). Because we were the only girls in the family, I remember thinking that losing Lois was worse for me than for my four brothers because I only had one sister. It took several years to realize this wasn't true.

I have recalled this dream often over the years, and it always brings me comfort. I would have to say that it has helped me to rise above my grief. Writing about it now, twenty-seven years later (in many ways, it seems like such a short time ago), feels good, but also, sad.

Comments

The dream, which comes just days after her beloved sister's funeral, begins with Rae-Ellen walking up an enclosed stairwell. In dreams, staircases usually symbolize increased spiritual awareness or a more transcendent perspective. The "enclosed" detail suggests protection. As the older of the two female siblings, Rae-Ellen might naturally feel protective of her younger sister. She certainly felt (at least at the onset of her grief) that her loss was more profound than that of her brothers. The enclosed staircase might also reflect some of the "closed" emotions associated with early grief (or *disarray*), such as denial and the need for solitude (see Chapter One).

Rae-Ellen climbs the staircase and enters an unfamiliar apartment. In dreams, dwellings, such as houses or apartments, usually represent the dreamer's circumstances. This strange apartment reflects Rae-Ellen's new and unfamiliar world of grief. But the odd apartment holds a happy surprise for Rae-Ellen: Lois, casually seated at the breakfast bar, has appeared to reassure her older sister that all would be well.

A breakfast bar is an interesting symbol. Without knowing Rae-Ellen's associations to her sister and breakfast bars, we know that dreams of meals are common in grief dreams. Meals provide nourishment and energy; symbolically, the dream is offering Rae-Ellen sustenance for her grief work.

In the next part of the dream, Rae-Ellen is able to ask her sister about her sudden, unexpected death, "Oh, Lowie, why did you have to die?" This is the question we all want to ask of those loved ones that we have lost. Why did they have to die? Where did they go? How could they have left us? It just doesn't seem right or fair.

In this particular dream, Lois responds in the objective, matter-of-fact way of dreams: "I needed to rest." She then goes on to offer Rae-Ellen a second reassurance, "Don't worry, [Russ and the girls will] be all right." Rae-Ellen hears these words and feels her sister's conviction: "She seemed to really know that they would."

Rae-Ellen confirms that the dream gave her a new, more spiritual perspective in the days following her sister's death. This is perhaps the central feature of all reassurance dreams.

How Rae-Ellen's Dream Helps Her

This dream arrived just days after Lois's death, giving Rae-Ellen timely reassurance and comfort. Rae-Ellen's dream helps her in four specific ways:

1. The dream serves as a protective shock absorber, allowing Rae-Ellen a way to manage her questions about the reason for her sister's sudden death and her concerns about her sister's husband and daughters.

2. This dream provides Rae-Ellen the opportunity to express her feelings with her poignant questions to her sister: "Oh, Lowie, why did you have to die?" "But what about Russ and the girls?" These painful questions are made more bearable by the answers

Lois provides: "I was just so tired. I needed to rest." "Don't worry, they'll be all right." The emotional effect of the dream was that Rae-Ellen felt right away "that my sister was OK and that I, too, would be OK."

3. Rae-Ellen's dream gives her the occasion for an intimate experience with her sister, just days after her death. This is an ideal internalized relationship—a very close relationship, even in death, that will help her resolve worry and doubt.

4. Rae-Ellen uses this dream "often during the next few years" as a reassuring bridge into her own future, helping her to "rise above" her grief. Now, twenty-seven years later, Rae-Ellen continues to call upon this dream for comfort and reassurance.

Toolbox: How Rae-Ellen's Dream Can Help You

Rae-Ellen tells us that in recalling her reassurance dream, she is better able to cope with the loss of her beloved sister. In this particular Toolbox, we'd like to focus on the concept of dream sharing. (Recall that Rae-Ellen's response to her dream was to "share the dream" with her brother-in-law.)

1. Dream sharing can help you with your grief work in the following ways:

- By sharing your dream, you will experience the reassurance of the dream with family and friends and receive the contact and support you need.

- By sharing your dream, you will reexperience the reassurance of the dream, allowing you to deepen and anchor the effect of the dream more securely for yourself.

- By sharing your dream, you will initiate dialogue with others who may offer you a particular perspective on your dream and perhaps share their dreams with you.

2. The fact that Rae-Ellen recalls this dream twenty-seven years later reminds us to consider the lifelong effect that grief dreams have on us and on future generations. We can calculate that twenty-seven years after this dream, Lois's daughters are now approximately the ages of Rae-Ellen and Lois at the time of Lois's death. We might imagine that Rae-Ellen and her nieces find renewed comfort and renewed perspective in a reassurance dream from a generation ago.

3. Recall a grief dream (or memory) that comforted you in the past. Bring that dream or memory to your awareness to comfort you now in your renewed grief. Share this reassuring dream with the family members and friends in your life now.

MARGE'S DREAM: TOUCHING TOM

In the dream, my entire family, except for my brother Tom (he had died), went shopping. Interestingly, my father, who passed away just a week after my brother, was alive and well in the dream. The shopping complex was large, with multiple buildings, and every kind of store. We ran up stairs and visited each store; we had a ball. We returned home, to my parents' house, and went down into the basement, which was the focal point for family activities. We decided to go back to the stores, and my Dad bought a tool. Again, we all had a delightful time. Once more, we returned to the basement, laughing and having a good time for the first time since Tom's death. Then, I looked over at my Dad's workbench area and saw Tom sitting in an old recliner. He was on his side with his head in his hand, watching us. He was laughing, without sound. I was the only person who saw him. I walked over to him and asked if he knew how much I loved him. He nodded and smiled and looked at me with much love in his eyes. I knew this was a dream. I asked if I could touch his hair, and again, he nodded. I reached out and actually felt his hair. I asked him if I could touch him again, and he nodded and smiled. I touched his face, and his skin felt warm and real. Then, the dream ended.

Feelings upon Waking

I woke up and cried. I felt the dream was a gift and I was grateful, but I wanted *more*.

The Back Story

My brother, Tom, died on February 20, 2003, in the Station Nightclub fire in West Warwick, Rhode Island. One hundred lives were lost in the blaze, and countless others were severely burned or injured.

I was seventeen when Tom was born. My other siblings were sixteen and fourteen. Tom was *our* baby. On his first night home from the hospital, the entire family got up for his middle-of-the-night feeding. He was truly adored by all of us. With all that love, it's no wonder he grew into such a wonderful human being.

Tom was funny, smart, loving, and hardworking. He gave long, loving hugs. You could see the love in his eyes when he looked at us.

One week after Tom's death, my father suffered a massive stroke, probably because of the tragedy of Tom's terrible death. In my dream, however, Dad was still alive. Perhaps my mind is having a difficult time accepting both losses at the same time.

I now find that I am concerned about how I will die—probably because of the way in which we lost Tom—but if death means that I will see my father and brother again, then that's OK.

Comments

Marge suffered the loss of her younger brother, Tom, in the horrific Station Nightclub fire, and her father, who suffered a massive stroke, just one week later. Marge, like Valerie, expresses her anguish over losing so much in such a short period of time. Families who have suffered multiple losses often withdraw to the safety of the family unit for prolonged periods of time. Most feel as if only other family members can truly understand the depth of their loss.

This need to withdraw is reflected in Marge's dream. The setting alternates briefly from shopping complex, to basement, back to shopping, and then finally, the dream remains fixed in the basement setting. This back-and-forth movement between shopping and basement sequences suggests that the family is now able to tolerate short periods of public exposure (symbolized by the vast shopping complex) but must then retreat to the security of the family circle (symbolized by the basement, which Marge describes as the hub of family activity). Given the media coverage surrounding the fire, Marge's family may have felt the need to withdraw more acutely.

The initial setting of the dream features Marge and her family (without Tom) happily shopping at a large shopping complex. Shopping (and spending money) is an energizing activity, perhaps reflecting the energy involved in grief work itself. Shopping dreams can also suggest a lack (when we shop, we search for something we need or want); what the family lacks, of course, is Tom, who is absent in the shopping scenes. This lack is affirmed by Marge's waking thoughts: "I wanted more."

The detail of the family's going back for more shopping is key. On the second trip, Marge's dad buys a tool. Remember that dreams often use key words to cue the dreamer. So we could say that this dream becomes a "tool" for Marge in two ways: the tool leads her to discover Tom, and then the dream itself becomes a tool for Marge to work on her grief as she absorbs both deaths.

The climax of the dream occurs when Marge sees Tom lying in an old recliner, in Dad's workbench area. The grief work is given a place in the dream that includes Dad and his workbench as well as Tom's reclining ease. So although this dream may at first seem to be only about Tom, it really addresses both losses.

Tom's reassuring presence—a presence only Marge can see—is an intimate, special gift. As in many of the dreams presented so far,

Tom is silent; he laughs without sound, smiles, and nods. Tom no longer communicates in the old way, with words, but in new ways, through a visual experience and then through physical sensations. (Compare with Susan's and Cory's dreams in Chapter Four.) This is the dream's way of showing Tom's new, internalized relationship with Marge.

But there are some familiar vestiges of the old Tom. The dream ends with a loving, tender exchange between sister and brother. Marge reminds Tom how much she loves him, and he "nodded and smiled and looked at me with much love in his eyes." This is the old Tom, who showed his love for his family in his eyes ("You could see the love in his eyes when he looked at us"). Marge then reaches out and touches first Tom's hair and then his face. He feels warm and real; just touching him again is especially reassuring for Marge, given Tom's traumatic death.

Marge is grateful for the dream and considers it a gift, but she wants more. Her desire for *more* reflects the innermost wish of all those who mourn: "I'd give anything for just one more day. If I had only known . . ." Although great comfort can be found in reassurance dreams such as Marge's, in truth, our loved ones are really never more than a thought away.

How Marge's Dream Helps Her

Marge is given a reassurance dream as a tool to help her cope with the death of her brother and father. More specifically, this dream helps Marge in the following ways:

1. Marge is able to sort through her positive feelings with her family and for Tom. In the first part of the dream, the family is able to gather and have "a ball" for the "first time since Tom's death." In the second part of the dream, Marge is able to experience Tom physically and conveys her love by touching him. Marge is also resolving anguished feelings by experiencing her brother as physically intact and restored. The dream also stim-

ulates a new feeling in Marge: after this dream she "wanted more." This is a common response to a dream—the desire for more dreams, more of what the dream provided, even if temporarily. Unfortunately, we can't predict the timing or sequencing of dreams. But we do know that more dreams will come, as the dreamers in this book demonstrate.

2. Marge builds an internalized relationship with her brother by experiencing him in a new, but wordless, way. He is silently present to her in the dreamscape. In his silent position on the recliner in her dad's workbench area, he is offering reassurance about his presence while at the same time helping her deal with her father's death.

3. Marge's dream is a bridge to her future in a way that is most common to early grief. She finds that she is concerned about how *she* will die. She then feels reassured that "if death means that I will see [Tom and Dad] again, then that's OK." Particularly in the early stages of grief, mourners often find great spiritual consolation in the idea that everyone will be together in an afterlife (or heaven). If thoughts of death persist, however, this may be a sign of depression or complicated bereavement, indicating the need for counseling (see Chapter Nine).

Toolbox: How Marge's Dream Can Help You

Dreams can be used as tools for providing reassurance. Marge's dream included her father's purchase of a tool and Tom's reclining in their father's workbench area as tools to help her with her grief. In this Toolbox, we will focus on a particular reassurance you would like to have and possible tools you might use to gain them.

1. Think for a moment and identify a particular reassurance you would like to have. For example, would you like a visual

reassurance of your loved one? Or perhaps you need reassurance that although you'll never be the person you were before your loss, you will, at some point, reclaim some measure of normality in your life. State your wish for a specific reassurance in one sentence.

2. Read through your grief dream journal to find a dream that speaks to your reassurance. If you do not find a relevant dream, or if you do not recall your dreams, ask family members and friends if they have had reassuring dreams. Often others' dreams can be as helpful as our own. In addition, the process of sharing a dream is a project that brings grievers together for contact and support. Pay careful attention to the details of the dreams that are reassuring. For example, do you *see* your loved one in a dream? That would provide a visual reassurance of your loved one. Or, in your dream, are you dressed or situated in a place that was at a time before your loss? This is your grief dream's way of showing you that somewhere in you the "normal" you still exists. Or does your deceased loved one appear in your cousin's dream, asking him to "tell everyone it will be all right." This way, you and your cousin can share the reassurance that is meant for "everyone."

3. Keep a list of the reassurances that these dreams provide. For example, you might write something like this: "My hairstyle in the dream was the one I had before my loss. So my dream is reminding me that the 'former me' still remains." Or you might write something like this: "My cousin described his dream where our uncle appeared looking tan and healthy, the way he looked the year before he died. We both felt so reassured, and I felt like I had the dream, too." The process of collecting dream reassurances will help you with your grief work by emphasizing the positive aspects of your relationship

with your loved one and by strengthening your ties with family and friends through shared dreams.

4. Remember that dreams are only one type of tool you can use to help you better cope with your grief. Can you think of other tools for reassurance? For example, you might share treasured memories, look at photographs and videos, and share your feelings with other family members, your grief partner, or a clergyperson. Explore how these other tools might help you in your loss.

JAN'S DREAM:
BEAU IN THE KITCHEN

My son Beau always enjoyed Thanksgiving with our large family. My kitchen seems to be the center of activity during the holidays, and it's usually packed with whoever can squeeze in. Everyone is always laughing and talking at once. In this dream, as usual, the kitchen was packed. The older kids, their spouses, and children were there along with the friends of the younger kids and any stray who didn't have a place to go that day. The chatter was all around and laughter rang out. I was feeling very relaxed and really good. Suddenly, I looked in the corner of the kitchen and there, perched on a bar stool, sat my son. He was not talking, but there was a big smile on his face, as if someone had just told him a funny story. He was just sitting there, listening and smiling. I got upset because he wasn't saying anything. My goal was to get him to talk, but it just wasn't happening. My dream ended at this point and I woke up.

Feelings upon Waking

I woke up in tears, feeling very frustrated and depressed. But after I reflected upon the dream, I felt consoled by it.

The Back Story

My son Beau died in May of 1999; he slipped and fell from the top of a waterfall while hiking with friends. He was eighteen. Beau was one of a kind. At an early age, he showed a unique personality and wittiness that kept us all laughing. He was very mature for his age and always used large and descriptive words when talking. He very much enjoyed even the most ordinary things.

He had many friends and loved reading. Beau especially enjoyed the outdoors, and some of his greatest times were spent camping with his buddies at the lake. Spring and fall were his favorite seasons, and Halloween was his favorite holiday. He enjoyed anything that bordered on the mysterious or paranormal.

This particular dream came in early November, and I was dreading the holiday season that year. I simply could not imagine how any of us would get through the next few months.

Although this dream initially made me feel sad and depressed, a few days later, I figured out that my son was telling me that nothing had changed. He was still around and enjoying the companionship of his family and friends, but now he was in the background. This made me feel a lot better and helped me through that first Thanksgiving without him.

We were all very fortunate to have had him in our lives, and though he only lived eighteen years, he lived life to the fullest. Sometimes I can still hear the echo of his laughter ring through the house. He has proven to us all—in different ways—that he is still around, just a breath away.

Comments

Like Susan's dream (Chapter Four), this is a holiday reassurance dream that answered Jan's dread of the first holiday season after her son's death. The dream gives her the usual kitchen scene, packed with family, filled with chatter and laughter. Then we see that in the dream Jan is feeling relaxed and good, unlike her conscious day world feeling of dread.

The appearance of Beau in the dream is a surprise to Jan: "Suddenly, I looked in the corner of the kitchen and there, perched on a bar stool, sat my son." Jan is upset in the dream because Beau doesn't speak. As we have seen, silent appearances of deceased loved ones are often unsettling for the dreamer because there is no spoken communication. (Recall Susan's dream of her daughter's signing but not speaking in Chapter Four.)

In Jan's dream, her "goal was to get him to talk but it just wasn't happening." Often our goals are different than the goal of the dream, and we feel frustrated until we get the symbolic point of the dream. The symbolic meaning is that Beau is near but different. In this case, Beau *looks* and smiles in his usual way, but he does not talk in his usual way. Or as Jan comes to understand, he was still around, "but now he was in the background." Dreams help us accept the reality of death while giving us a new perspective.

Understanding the symbolic meaning of a dream takes time, as Jan reminds us. She explains that it wasn't until "a few days later" that she figured out the meaning of the dream for her. This is an example of how dreams work on us over time to bring meaning. When Jan first woke up, she felt frustrated and depressed. Days later, she understood and accepted that now Beau was in the background. Jan says, "This made me feel a lot better and helped me through that first Thanksgiving without him."

How Jan's Dream Helps Her

Losing a child—at any age and under any circumstances—is an immeasurable tragedy. Jan speaks for most bereaved persons, and in particular bereaved parents, when she voices her concerns about coping with the approaching holidays. Her son, she tells us, was especially fond of the fall, and we can only imagine the additional surge of grief that Jan must experience when the leaves change color and begin to fall each year. Once again, we see a connection to the Thanksgiving holiday. (See Katherine's dream in Chapter Three.) Approaching holidays often herald an increase in grief dreams that bring comfort and hope to the bereaved. Jan's Thanksgiving dream of Beau does this in the following specific ways:

1. Holiday dreams can help the dreamer absorb the shock of anniversary events after the loss of a loved one. These grief dreams also help the dreamer accept the loss with new perspective. By understanding that Beau was now "in the background," Jan was accepting the reality of Beau's death in the context of the first family holiday without him.

2. Jan courageously sorts through and works through difficult feelings in this dream. Initially, she feels "frustrated and depressed" that she wasn't able to get Beau to talk. Then over time, she is able to accept the meaning of the dream, "feel a lot better," and cope with the family holiday.

3. Jan is developing an internalized relationship with Beau through this dream, understanding that he "was still around . . . but now he was in the background."

Toolbox: How Jan's Dream Can Help You

Jan's dream shows us how to deal with a reassurance dream that initially appears to be sad and depressing. Often dreamers awake with feelings of frustration and depression. In the dream, Jan couldn't get Beau to talk. Consequently, she focused on what *wasn't* happening in her dream, and as a result, she felt depressed and frustrated. When she shifted her perspective and began to focus on what *was* happening in the dream, she was able to experience the positive and reassuring effect of the dream. The following are some helpful suggestions for coping with dreams that provoke negative reactions at first:

1. If you awake feeling upset by a dream because it didn't go the way you wanted, focus on the objective plot of the dream. Try not to think about what you wanted to have happen. Eliminate the goal you have imposed on the dream.

2. Stay objective. Retell the dream to yourself or to someone else exactly as it happened, without interpretation or wishes. Jung said that dreams show the situation as it is rather than what we wish it to be. In Jan's case, Beau was perched in the kitchen smiling, and Jan was relaxed and feeling good. Beau does not talk, and Jan can't make him talk. But the dream says that Beau "was still around . . . but now he was in the background." Often in the retelling of the dream to someone else in an objective way, you can see what the dream is, rather than what it is not. In Jan's case, she was able to realize, just a few days later, that her dream was in fact reassuring.

3. When you discover what your dream is, write this down in your grief dream journal.

There are three things that can be said about all reassurance dreams: they are complex, consoling, and always connected to a particular question or concern of the dreamer. In this way, reassurance dreams can be powerful self-help tools during bereavement. Of course, we believe that *all* grief dreams are ultimately helpful to mourners, including the most dreaded type of grief dream, the trauma dream, to which we now turn.

6

The Trauma Dream

*Deep into that darkness peering, long I stood there
wondering,
fearing,
Doubting, dreaming dreams no mortals ever dared
to dream before.*

Edgar Allan Poe, *The Raven*

"M y roommate, Ryan, was killed in a car accident when we were seniors in college," says Thomas. "At first, I had some very scary and graphic dreams of the accident and his injuries; but as time passed, the nightmares faded, and now I rarely dream of him at all. I still think of him all the time, though."

Thomas's disturbing dreams appeared shortly after Ryan's death, but it's not at all unusual for mourners to experience trauma dreams at any time—even many years after the loss. Trauma dreams come in many forms, ranging from the graphic and grisly, like Thomas's accident dreams of Ryan, to a more subdued, understated terror, such as a strange sound or a dark figure lurking in the background.

HOW TRAUMA DREAMS CAN HELP US

Of course, not all grieving people experience trauma dreams, but among those who do, most agree that trauma dreams are ultimately

119

helpful in their journey of grief. But how can something that scares you be helpful?

Trauma dreams can be helpful in several ways. First, trauma dreams can help us accept the reality of our loss. "A few months after our daughter died of SIDS, I had a dream," says Mary. "In the dream, a stranger kidnapped Haylee and took her to a foreign country. I knew we'd never see her again. I woke up screaming. Until then, it wasn't real to me; but that night, I knew for certain I'd never see her again."

Second, trauma dreams can help us work through the various feelings and emotions (some of which we've never felt before) that come with profound loss. "My husband turned into a hideous monster in the dream," says Tanya. "It was terrifying, but he was so abusive in life, I thought that maybe the dream was trying to get me to look at who he really was—not the idealized version I made him out to be now that he's dead."

Finally, trauma dreams can help us with the painful adjustment process as we learn to live in a world without our loved one. "A few months after my friend Maury died of a heart attack," says Jerry, "I had a nightmare about him. I was standing on the sidewalk, peering down a dark alley. Suddenly, I saw Maury. His back was to me and I yelled to get his attention. He turned and looked at me but wouldn't talk to me. He just hurried down the alley and disappeared. I ran after him, screaming for him to come back, but he didn't seem to hear me. I felt terrible."

Of course, the defining characteristic of a trauma dream is that it traumatizes the dreamer, at least initially. This brings us to perhaps the most surprising aspect of trauma dreams in the context of grief: despite the terror associated with these dreams, more often than not, bereaved dreamers eventually come to view their trauma dreams positively.

Trauma dreams (and grief dreams in general) not only help us accept the reality of the loss, sort through our feelings, and adjust to the death, but they also aid in meaning making. As discussed in Chapters One and Two, meaning making is a creative response to profound loss. This response helps us begin to rebuild our lives and can serve as a bridge for reentering the world after a period of intense bereavement.

"My early dreams of Elliot were scary hospital dreams," says Nathan. "I would be back in the room with him, watching him sleep, terrified he would stop breathing. He was bald and emaciated, the way he looked just before he died. Sometimes he would die in the dream; other times, I would walk into the room and find him dead with his eyes open. These dreams were terrifying, but they also reminded me that I was *there*—I stayed even when I wanted to be anyplace other than that hospital—I was there until the end."

Nathan's love and loyalty—his refusal to abandon Elliot—are conveyed through his trauma dreams. Nathan's dreams highlight the positive and meaningful aspects of his grief: Nathan did all that he could; he was steadfast and caring; he stayed until the end.

We have found, moreover, that nearly all trauma dreams either contain a small kernel of hope or at the very least point the dreamer in a hopeful direction. In this way, trauma dreams are ultimately healing. As you read the following trauma dreams, ask yourself how the dreamer might find meaning and healing through his or her dream.

FRANK'S DREAM: MY FATHER'S REACH

In the dream, I was in a plowed, smoky field with my father. He's dying and reaching out to me. I am aware that he is already dead in the dream and that he wants to drag me into his world. I am filled with terror.

Feelings upon Waking

I woke up in a sweat, heart pounding, and breathless. It took me several minutes to settle down, but there was no more sleep that night.

The Back Story

In the summer of 1970, I saw Federico Fellini's film *Satyricon*. The film had a profoundly disturbing effect on me, and I'm still haunted by many of its images. In one unforgettable scene, the impoverished old poet, Eumolpus, is lying on a plowed, smoky field, close to death (he thinks), leaving a kind of oral will to the young man, Encolpius, to whom he had been a kind of mentor or father figure. This film obviously influenced my dream.

When I had this dream, my father had already been dead for over ten years. There had never been any tenderness between us while he lived. In fact, I do not recall his ever touching me, except in violence. So his reaching out to me in the dream must have brought up intense feelings of fear and memories of his rages.

Many years ago in therapy, I learned that it is not the dream that determines the feeling, but the feeling that creates the dream. Perhaps, had my father lived longer, we might have moved beyond our "stranger status," and my dreams of him would not be so filled with terror.

Comments

Frank's dream shows the importance of the dreamer's back story in understanding the dream. That is, when we read the dream in the full context of Frank's reactions and associations, we can better decipher the dream's meaning. Frank's feelings upon waking indicate that the dream is deeply unsettling to him.

Equally unsettling is Frank's relationship with his father. We first met Frank in Chapter Three, as he shared his uplifting visitation dream about his mother. It is clear from Frank's back story that his relationship with his father differed greatly from the one he shared with his mother—a difference that is reflected in the dream.

Frank was only fourteen when his father died, and he tells us that he was fearful of his father's rages and violent actions; understandably, his father's reaching out to him in the dream is perceived as threatening.

So far, Frank's dream is a traumatic nightmare, recollecting his father's anger as well as his own fear; but there is a complex twist to the dream. Frank draws a connection between his dream and a scene in *Satyricon*. At first, we see a stark contrast between the two father-son relationships: the movie portrays a father figure reaching out in loving farewell to a young man; but when Frank's father reaches out to him in the dream, Frank is terrified.

If we probe more deeply, however, and consider Frank's comments, we understand what Freud meant when he described dreams as wish fulfillments. Frank writes, "Perhaps, had my father lived longer, we might have moved beyond our 'stranger status,' and my dreams of him would not be so filled with terror." This statement, combined with Frank's association of the Fellini film with his dream, expresses Frank's wish for a better relationship with his abusive father.

How Frank's Dream Helps Him

Frank's trauma dream helps him deal with the reality of his father's death, as he attempts to reconcile the difficult relationship they shared. More specifically, Frank's dream helps him in the following ways:

1. His dream helps him continue to absorb the shock of his father's death, which he experienced at the vulnerable age of fourteen. Adolescents often repress their grief until adulthood, when they are mature enough to bear the difficult feelings. So it is understandable that Frank would have this dream at age twenty-four, when he could more fully process the fears and unfulfilled wishes left by his father's death.

2. Frank uses this dream to continue to work out his ambivalent feelings for his father. This dream highlights Frank's fear of his father as well as his wish for a better leave-taking with his father. Freud observed that fears in dreams also express wishes.

3. Frank's dream helps him with his inner relationship with his father. Through his association to the Fellini film, Frank asserts his yearning for a more generative, loving father. Over time, trauma dreams offer insight and purpose for the dreamer. Through this dream—and through subsequent dreams—Frank might be able to gain a deeper understanding of his father and perhaps a sense of reconciliation and peace.

Toolbox: How Frank's Dream Can Help You

Jung wrote that dreams complement and compensate our lives. Trauma dreams—like Frank's—can, with time and grief work, provide hopeful redemption. Frank's dream also reminds us that some relationships are more complicated than others, and the more complex the relationship, the more complex the grieving. With this in mind, Frank's dream can help you in the following ways:

1. Frank's dream shows how his troubled relationship with his father is present in his terrifying dream, even ten years after his father's death. Such an unsettling nightmare about a difficult relationship may be hard to bear alone. If you, too, are having trauma dreams, reading this book and keeping a grief dream journal can be helpful first steps.

2. Consider sharing your dreams, fears, and ambivalent feelings with your grief partner, trusted friend, family member, or pastor.

3. If your trauma dreams persist, consider engaging the help of a counselor. Frank explains in his back story that he worked on his dreams in therapy. Counseling can be an invaluable tool for traumatic dreams of traumatic relationships.

- In particular, if you have had an abusive relationship with the person you are now grieving, we strongly urge you to seek a therapist to help you. With counseling, intense, ambivalent feelings will be explored and made bearable.

- Contact your primary care physician, pastor, or local mental health center for the name of a psychotherapist to help you with your grief and your grief dreams. Refer to the Reader Resources section of this book for help in locating a competent therapist or counselor.

NADINE'S DREAM: THE FIRE

I had this recurring dream following the deaths of my brother and father. The dream takes place in the finished basement of my home. There is a fire raging in another part of the house, and I am trying to pick up and carry my kitty cats, both at the same time, but they keep getting out of my arms; I can't seem to hold on to them. I'm screaming, telling my father and brother, "Come on! We've got to go now!" I keep screaming. They yell back at me with angry looks on their faces. I can't quite make out what they are saying, and tears start to roll down my cheeks. They absolutely must come with me; it's imperative! But they seem to be telling me that they cannot come with me—that I have to go by myself—and they must stay behind. At the point where I'm most traumatized, I wake up.

Feelings upon Waking

I woke up crying.

The Back Story

I lost both my brother and father in a rather short period of time. My younger brother, James, committed suicide two weeks before his thirtieth birthday. His death devastated me and literally changed my life. I have never been quite the same since.

Less than two years later, my father died after suffering a series of strokes and heart attacks. All of these occurred after my brother's

death. My father was from the "old school," where a man's firstborn
son means everything. Dad was quite depressed after James died,
and I think his depression contributed to his death.

I also lost twin cats, both of whom I raised from kittens. They
lived for twenty years and had been my "children" for most of my
life. Losing them has been very painful because they were so depen-
dent on me, and I felt as if I had let them down. (I had to—in the
end—have them put to sleep.)

For a long time, I thought of this recurring dream as a nightmare, but as time passes, I have come to view this dream in a more
positive light. I think that my brother and father—and even my
cats—were trying to tell me that they can no longer come with me.
I have to go on with my life—and my journey of grief—alone.

Comments

The dream begins in Nadine's basement. In dreams, basements often symbolize the stability and health of the dreamer. Basements are
a place where things are stored and can be found if you look for
them; they are also symbolic of knowledge kept below our conscious
awareness. Basements are also common settings for grief dreams.
(See Marge's dream in Chapter Five.)

Nadine expresses some very intense feelings in the dream. Tears
of grief and frustration roll down her face as she frantically picks up
her cats and screams to her father and brother to get out of the
burning house. On a more symbolic level, fire in dreams usually represents intense, "burning" feelings, such as anger. Fire is also a situation where one must take a course of action. Here we can see the
purpose of the dream.

Nadine must get out of the house; but her father and brother
cannot come with her. Her difficult course of action in the dream
is that she has to go alone, emphasizing the necessary course of
action in her life without her father and brother, and even her cats,
who slip from her grasp, adding to the trauma of the dream.

Nadine's dream vividly describes her trauma while at the same time offering her an honest perspective: she must indeed move on with her life without her loved ones.

How Nadine's Dream Helps Her

Nadine initially classifies her recurring trauma dream as a nightmare. As her grief matures, however, she is able to recognize the healing aspects of her dreams. Nadine's dream helps her in the following specific ways:

1. Through the dream, Nadine is able to absorb the shock of the suicide of her brother and the subsequent death of her father.

2. Nadine is able to sort through her feelings. Initially, she feels a frustrated desire to save her father, brother, and cats. When this fails, she feels distraught at the realization that she must go on without them.

3. The dream provides an understanding of her father and brother that will be a foundation for an internalized relationship: they are adamant that they cannot come with her. Although this is not a comforting communication, her brother and father tell her the truth, and the truth is fundamental to any developing relationship.

4. The dream can be a bridge from Nadine's past, to the present, and to the future. In the dream, she faces the deaths of her brother and father; she experiences the disarray of her emotions; and she hears the hard truth of her future: she must go on alone.

Toolbox: How Nadine's Dream Can Help You

Nadine's dream is an example of a recurring trauma dream. Often, when the death of a loved one is sudden and unexpected, these dreams repeat over and over again to absorb the shock of the death. Although the dreamer may feel trauma-tized by the dream, the effect on the grief work is usually pos-itive. These dreams prepare the dreamer, while sleeping, for the daytime reality of the death of the loved one. Such dreams may also describe the current attitude of the dreamer and sug-gest a course of action, as we have seen with the fire situation in Nadine's dream. This Toolbox focuses on suggestions for understanding and coping with recurrent trauma dreams.

1. As we stressed with Frank's dream, trauma dreams can be intensely unsettling. We again remind you to share your dreams with your grief partner and consider seeking the help of a grief counselor. (Chapter Nine includes a section on Seek-ing Professional Help. See also the Reader Resources section of this book.)

2. To understand your dream, focus on the details of the set-ting of the dream. The setting suggests the inner situation of the dreamer. For example, Nadine's dream setting was the fin-ished basement of her home, where there is a fire raging.

- Describe the setting of your dream with a personal state-ment, such as, "I am in my living room with a fierce dog by my side."

- Write down your personal associations to each element of the setting, using this simple format: *living room:* where I am most comfortable and see visitors; *fierce dog by my side:* protective of me, just like my childhood dog, Spike.

- Consult your dream dictionary to see if there are fur-ther elaborations on the setting elements that might trigger an association that you've missed.

- Remember to use your dream dictionary only as a guide, discarding dictionary notations that don't seem to fit your feel of the dream.

3. Consider how this setting may describe your present situation and then creatively envision a possible course of action.

- For example, you might identify the situation this way: "I need to pay more attention to the Spike figure. He's reminding me to protect myself against the intrusive visitors, who keep telling me I should 'be over it' by now."

- In naming this, you might come up with the following self-help action: "I need to reach out to others who understand my loss and enlist their 'protection.' I should simplify and focus on more 'dog-friendly' activities, such as exercise and regular meals."

- Let your associations to your dream symbols guide you to the meaning of the dream.

ARLENE'S DREAM:
A MAN AT THE DOOR

In the dream, it is night and very dark outside. I hear some very scary sounds coming from beyond my front door. I go to the door and discover that someone is trying to get into the house. I hold the door shut, but the person continues to push on it. I can't see who it is because it's dark. I feel frantic. Then, I think that it is my brother, Rich, and now I want to open the door but cannot. My eldest daughter is asleep upstairs, and my two youngest children (who are all adults now) appear in the dream as young children. They are in the front room. They cry out and try to open the front windows. They finally open the windows and jump out. They *see a figure on the porch and run toward the figure, calling, "Uncle Richie, Uncle Richie!" He holds out his hands and tells them to stop. "Stay there," he says. "Don't come any closer." At this point, I climb out of the window, too, but Rich holds up his hands to stop me from coming to him. I tell him to come in and talk to me, but he goes away.*

Feelings upon Waking

During the dream, I was scared. Everything was so dark, and someone was trying to break into my home. Later, however, I felt relaxed and peaceful.

The Back Story

My brother, Rich, had not been in the best of health, but his condition did not seem to be life threatening. Over the course of a year, however, he gradually deteriorated and eventually died of liver failure. I felt guilty because I did not spend the last hours with him and instead went to a baby shower. I really did not want to go to the shower, but Rich encouraged me to go. He sounded cheerful the last time we spoke.

When he died, I could not get through the grief and sorrow. I've dreamed of him many times and always woke up crying. Despite some of the scary aspects of this dream, I've been very comforted and consoled by it.

I think of him often and pray for him nightly. I miss him very much; we were very close. But I think I'll dream of him again and hope he'll reassure me of his new, pain-free life. This hope gives me comfort. And my faith has strengthened because I know that he is with God.

Comments

Arlene's dream begins at night, with someone trying to get into her home. She reacts defensively, holding the door shut to keep the intruder out. This action reflects the instinct to "shut the door" to new experiences, common in early grief.

Arlene feels safe and protected inside her home (or, symbolically, inside herself) and defends against intrusive thoughts and feelings. This is a healthy response in early grief. But then, a shift occurs. Arlene suddenly has a thought: the person behind the door is Rich. Now she wants to open the door but cannot.

The push-and-pull action of the dream reflects the work of our psychological defenses; when we feel vulnerable, we put up defenses that are not easily surmounted unless we have assistance. Arlene alone cannot open the door; her "assistance" comes in the form of two of her adult children, who appear now as young children. Children represent spontaneous, hopeful qualities that find new openings for our deepest wishes. Arlene's children find such an opening, through the windows, and Arlene is able to make contact with Rich. Arlene's wish comes true: Rich has appeared to console her.

But the wish comes with some new qualifications. As we have seen with other grief dreams, the deceased appears the same, yet different. Rich can appear in dreams, he can offer consolation, but he demands distance. Still, he *is* available to Arlene, but in a different way. She seems to accept the new conditions of their relationship and feels a sense of consolation and peace.

How Arlene's Dream Helps Her

Arlene's dream is an example of how a dream initially may be frightening but then turns out to be comforting. Her dream helps her in the following specific ways:

1. The dramatic beginning of the dream serves as a way for Arlene to absorb the shock of Rich's death. The dream also helps her adjust to the reality of his death by showing how Rich is now different.

2. Arlene uses the dream to sort through her feelings of sorrow and guilt about the circumstances of her brother's death. The push-and-pull of the dream door suggests the back-and-forth

interplay of grief with guilt. Once the window is opened, Arlene can "air out" her guilt and allow a realistic, new sense of restrained, but "relaxed and peaceful," contact with her brother.

3. Arlene develops an inner relationship with her brother through this dream. She feels he will appear to her again to reassure her.

4. Arlene indicates that the dream has provided her with a sense of renewal for her own life in that the dream served to strengthen her faith.

Toolbox: How Arlene's Dream Can Help You

The meaning of Arlene's dream is discovered by focusing on the plot of the dream. Jung called this the *dramatic structure* of the dream. Breaking down the dream into dramatic segments can be particularly helpful in trauma dreams because it helps the dreamer feel less fearful about the dream. Using Arlene's dream, this Toolbox demonstrates how to identify the dramatic structure of a trauma dream as a tool for understanding your own trauma dream.

There are three basic steps involved in analyzing the dramatic structure of your trauma dreams: *diagram, assess, ask*.

1. *Diagram.* Diagram your dream into plot segments that describe the main parts of the action:

- Arlene shuts the door to the intruder. → Arlene cannot open the door to Rich. → The children find and open the windows to meet Rich. → Arlene meets a same-but-different Rich.

2. *Assess.* Review each plot segment and ask how this dramatizes your current situation.

- For example, in the first segment of her dream plot, Arlene might ask, "How in my life am I closing doors? What do I fear is intruding on me?"

- In the second segment, she might ask, "How is it difficult for me to open doors for myself?" Often the symbolic meaning of key elements of the plot, such as open and closed doors, becomes clear when we simply ask the question.

- In the third segment of the dream, the children discover the solution of opening the front windows and finding Rich. By consulting a dream dictionary, the symbolic meaning of *children* could be understood as those spontaneous, creative, and nonguilty aspects of Arlene's personality.

- In the fourth segment, Arlene meets a same-but-different Rich. She might assess how this transformed view of Rich is important in her grief work, particularly the way in which it affects her spiritual life.

3. *Ask*. Dreamers should ask, "How does this show my current situation? What helpful meaning can I draw from this symbolic dream drama?" So Arlene might ask herself, "How can I find and use childlike qualities to help me grieve?" She might focus less on her guilt and more on her hopeful sense of inner contact with Rich, which the dream drama provides.

RUDY'S DREAM: LOSING BILL

Cheap, tattered Christmas decorations hung from the exposed pipes running the length of the subway tunnel. They were supposed to be festive, but for me, they accentuated the gloominess of the city. It must have been New York, because just being there depressed me.

Bill and I had to move quickly to make our connection. We had to move with the masses to the next train. Bill looked back at me as I got ready to follow his lead. I could tell he was mapping out the route in his head so that we wouldn't get separated. My heart ached. I knew he was sick, and this place could make even healthy people feel sick. I would move quickly when the train pulled into the next station so that I could stay in control. I would make it better.

Finally, after what seemed like an eternity of bumping and churning among a sea of zombielike strangers, the train lurched to a stop. When the doors screeched open with a jerk, the crowd was ready. We all lunged forward at the same time, some pushing left, and some pushing right. No one looking up from the quiet solitude they had created in their heads. Bill glanced back at me one more time to make sure I was OK. He always cared, and he didn't like this place any more than I did, despite its Christmas decorations.

As he rushed forward to the next tunnel, he was suddenly engulfed by the crowd. Even though I pushed to stay with him, only a short step behind, the crowd was too strong for us. It swallowed Bill up. And suddenly, I remembered he was sick. I needed to make it all better and I couldn't keep up. I glanced up at the decorations and realized that this may be our last Christmas together, ever. No. There was more—he was gone. Bill wasn't sick anymore. He was dead.

Feelings upon Waking

I did feel relief that I finally had my first dream of my husband, even though waking up was almost like losing him all over again.

The Back Story

As a person who loves to write, I got up immediately and recorded my thoughts. What follows are my exact words from that morning in June 1995:

I had been very fearful of seeing my husband again in a dream. When I awoke after this dream, I experienced a small amount of relief that it had finally happened. I see in the dream that I had this burning desire to make things right for my husband, and despite my efforts to try and fix things while he was ill, the cancer swallowed him up anyway. My husband died two weeks before Christmas, which explains the Christmas decorations in the dream. Neither of us were big fans of New York, and years earlier, when I was in college, I had had a very frightening experience on the subway.

I spent the last six days at my husband's side at the hospital. Finally, nurses told me I had to go home and get some sleep, as I was on the verge of exhaustion. As I slept that night, a bright light woke me. It came through one of my windows and bathed me in an incredible sense of peace. As I lay back down, the hospital called to say my husband was gone. As a Christian, I know that was my husband's last good-bye, as Jesus or perhaps an angel carried him home. That remembrance of what that light felt like has brought incredible peace and comfort to my kids and me.

Comments

We are fortunate to have Rudy's immediate recollection of her trauma dream from her grief journal. Rudy, like many mourners, expresses apprehension about seeing her husband in a dream. The fear of dreams is common in early grief and seems to be connected to fear of revisiting the trauma of the death. Even though we know that dreams help us absorb the shock of death and impress upon us the reality of our loss, these initial dreams are often quite dreadful.

The symbolic aspects of the dream, so well amplified by Rudy, set the traumatic scene. It is Christmas, the season of Bill's death, and they are in a New York subway, the scene of another frightening experience for Rudy during her college years.

The conclusion or goal of the dream comes when the crowd swallows up Bill, invoking the horrible images of the cancer that consumed him. The crowd, like the cancer that took Bill's life, is impersonal and overwhelming. Despite her burning desire to make things better and Bill's strong lead, there is no stopping the crowd (cancer). Try as she might to save him—to make things better— Rudy and Bill are no match for this crowd (cancer).

How Rudy's Dream Helps Her

Rudy's insight from the conclusion of this dream will be to understand Bill's cancer as an uncontrollable force, "too strong for us." She must mourn her impossible desire to keep Bill by her side in light of the overwhelming power of the crowd (cancer). Over time, she will likely come to see the dream as an opening for her to develop an inner relationship with her husband. Rudy's dream helps her in the following concrete ways:

1. The dream helps her absorb the shock of Bill's death and impresses upon her the reality of her loss. Although this reality is difficult for Rudy to bear, she uses the dream to work on her grief.

2. Rudy sorts through her feelings in the dream. She is aware that she has a "burning desire to make things right" for her husband and that she was unable to fulfill that desire; both she and Bill are overpowered.

3. The dream provides an opening for Rudy to develop a continuing relationship with Bill. Twice in the dream, Bill looks back at her to make sure she is OK. Rudy may be able to build on these dream-clips of Bill's protective reassurance to further develop her inner relationship with him.

Toolbox: How Rudy's Dream Can Help You

In early grief, like Rudy, we may fear our dreams; we may even try to avoid sleep. Rudy's fear of dreaming of Bill alerts us to the importance of sleep. Restful sleep, although elusive for many, is essential during mourning, as sleep deprivation can actually exacerbate grief symptoms. Try to monitor the number of hours you are sleeping each day to ensure adequate rest, not only for your mental and emotional well-being but also because studies have shown that grieving people are more susceptible to illness.

Consider recording sleep details as part of your grief dream journal, and if, over a period of a week, you are averaging fewer than four to five hours of sleep in a twenty-four-hour period, it is important to consult your primary care physician. Now let us turn to the focus of this Toolbox: searching for the *dream goal*.

Rudy's dream shows us yet another way to understand a grief dream: by examining the conclusion or *goal* of the dream. In Rudy's dream, the goal of the dream was to show the overpowering force of Bill's cancer. This method of dreamwork is achieved by mastering three easy steps, explained here in detail:

1. Summarize your trauma dream (in a few short sentences) with a focus on the ending of the dream. Rudy might summarize her dream this way: "I needed to make it all better and I couldn't keep up. The crowd was too strong for us; it swallowed Bill up."

2. Amplify the main symbols using your own associations and a dream dictionary. Using your summary, amplify the main symbols in the dream. Rudy would think about her associations to the "crowd swallowing Bill" and would conclude that the crowd might symbolize the cancer that indeed "swallowed up" her husband.

3. Consider the goal of the dream: How does the *ending* of the dream offer you important information for your grief work? Rudy considers how the ending (or goal) of her trauma dream helps her with her grief work. She sees the dream as helping her to face the fact that despite her best efforts, she could not save Bill.

4. Here's another dream summary for practice: "I watch in shock as a man chops down a beautiful oak tree in my backyard.

He tells me matter-of-factly that it was a necessary sacrifice. I realize I now have a beautiful view of the ocean."

The *goal* of the dream is a view of the ocean, which is made possible by the shocking sacrifice of the oak tree. The main symbol is the sacrificed oak tree. Once the symbol of the sacrificed oak tree is amplified, the goal of the dream (a beautiful view of the ocean) can be considered in the ways it furthers the grief work.

In this particular dreamer's case, the oak tree represents the dreamer's hard determination ("hard as oak") to keep her deceased mother's home (featuring oak beams) despite a bitter family controversy and excessive estate taxes. Once she was able to relinquish her hold on the house and "let it fall," she was able to have a more peaceful life ("view of the ocean" equals a peaceful life).

In the midst of profound loss, our dreams, including trauma dreams, help us express and explore our innermost emotions so that we can creatively envision a new relationship with our deceased loved one. Trauma dreams, like all grief dreams, help us accept and adjust to our loss.

In addition to the four main categories of grief dreams—visitation, message, reassurance, and trauma dreams—there are other types of grief dreams, which are best discussed separately. Let us now explore these other types of grief dreams.

7

Other Types of Grief Dreams

*Dreams say what they mean, but they don't say it in
daytime language.*

Gail Godwin

As we move beyond our examination of the four most common
grief dream types—visitation, message, reassurance, and
trauma—you have probably come to recognize the important role
your dreams play in helping you to cope with your grief. It's our
hope, moreover, that you now feel more confident in working with
your dreams, using some of the techniques described in the Toolboxes. Although the final three chapters of this book will depart
from the format of Chapters Three through Six, we will continue
the practice of providing Toolboxes as needed.

At this point, you may be asking, "What if my grief dream
doesn't seem to fit any of the four grief dream types discussed so far?"
We want to reemphasize that our classification of the four most
common types of grief dreams is intended to serve only as a framework for understanding your grief dreams. We fully recognize that
some dreams fall outside this basic framework and that certain grief
dreams may contain elements of more than one core dream type.
For example, Katherine's dream of her grandfather (in Chapter
Three), classified by us as a visitation dream, also contains elements
of reassurance. Katherine explicitly points us to this reality in her

back story: "He [Grandpa] visits me to remind me that he is still with me."

Another example of these *combination dreams* is Alberto's dream of his mother, Rita. Notice how the dream begins as a trauma dream but then has elements of visitation, message, and reassurance dreams:

"My mother died when I was twenty-one. She, my dad, and my younger brother were camping out when the portable gas grill my mom was using exploded in her face. Mom died from her injuries about a week after the accident. Several weeks after she died, she came to me in a dream. I was sitting on the front steps of our old brownstone, and I saw her standing across the street. At first, I was terrified because I was afraid that she would look bad, like she did after the accident. I tried to run away in the dream but couldn't move. Mom crossed the street, and I got a good look at her. She looked normal. She sat beside me on the stoop, and we just sat there without saying a word. I woke up happy, with tears running down my face."

Alberto's dream reminds us that many grief dreams can be classified as combination dreams, because many have at least some elements from more than one core category. Indeed, you have probably come to understand what the dream experts know well: every dream is unique. And any generalization may cause us to miss the distinctive features of a particular dream. In short, your grief dream does not need to be typecast to be helpful.

OTHER TYPES OF GRIEF DREAMS

In addition to both the core and combination dreams are other types of grief dreams, including these: intentional dreams, lucid dreams, and daydreams, as well as series and prophetic dreams, which are far more common and therefore warrant a more detailed explanation.

Intentional Dreams

How many times have you longed for a dream of your deceased loved one? If you're like most mourners, you probably welcome your grief dreams and view them as treasured gifts. Often, simply reconnecting with our loved ones through the dreamscape—seeing them again, perhaps hearing their voice or the sound of their laughter, and even touching them—can help us during those particularly difficult "grief days" that mourners know so well. The good news is, sometimes, it is possible to ask for and receive a dream.

When Kat lost her father in a car accident, she longed for a sign that would reassure her that her father was OK. "Frequently, at night before I went to bed, I'd ask my dad in a prayer to show me he was still with me," says Kat. "Two months later, my dad came to me in a dream. I was so happy to see him. I can't tell you how good I felt. It was like relief had poured into my body." Kat shows us that saying a short prayer is one way to state your intention or desire for a dream. Although her dream might also be categorized as a visitation dream, Kat's repeated prayers for a dream—prayers that are ultimately answered—classify this dream as an intentional dream.

Like Kat, Lynn desperately wanted a dream to reconnect her with her deceased loved one. "After my twin sister's funeral," says Lynn, "I lay down for a nap, asking for a dream that would bring Maren back to me. I just needed to see her again. Maren appeared in my dream, wearing our favorite outfit, with her hand raised in a high five. I woke up with my hand in the air, catching her high five." Although Lynn certainly received a powerful message from her sister, her purposeful, presleep thoughts help define her dream as intentional.

Prayers, wishful thoughts, or affirming statements, such as, "I want my mother to come to me in a dream," are all ways that dreamers can help initiate a dream. Valerie's dream (in Chapter Five) is another example of an intentional dream that answered the fervent question she had posed before falling asleep. If you're interested in working on an intentional dream yourself, see Valerie's Toolbox to review techniques for intentional dreaming.

Lucid Dreams

Many dream books describe an experience known as lucid dreaming. These are dreams in which the dreamer is aware of dreaming while still asleep. During the rapid eye movement (REM) sleep phase, in which dreaming most often occurs, lucid dreamers may be able to recall information from their waking state as well as control the outcome of their dreams. Clinical dream literature describes the successful use of lucid dreaming in the treatment of recurrent nightmares.

Gwen, for example, was plagued with nightmares about her deceased, abusive husband, Joe. She explains the lucid dream she had after two years of intensive psychotherapy: "I saw my dead husband approach me angrily. I knew I was dreaming, and I knew what I needed to do. I looked him in the eye and said, 'Joe, you can't hurt me now. And you need to apologize.' He stopped and nodded sadly, saying, 'I'm so sorry, Gwen.'"

Gwen demonstrates the benefits of lucid dreaming within the overall context of therapy. Our caution for grieving individuals is that lucid control over a dream might suppress emotions and insights that are essential to the grief process. For example, if Rudy (see Chapter Six) had lucidly changed the ending of her subway dream, she would have missed an opportunity to realize the inevitable outcome of her husband's cancer. However, we do agree that the use of lucid dreams at carefully selected therapeutic moments can be empowering for the dreamer when assisted by an experienced psychotherapist (see the Reader Resources section).

Daydreams

For those who do not recall their dreams, daydreaming can be a useful tool for grief work. Daydreams are defined as thoughts and images, usually pleasant, that pass through the mind while awake.

Daydreams may come spontaneously or may be purposefully produced during a relaxed, conscious state. Daydreams are often the by-product of meditation or some other type of induced relaxation.

Louise describes how her use of daydreaming steadied her in the months following her son's motorcycle accident:

"At first, all day, I just kept seeing Alex the way he looked at the morgue—it was unbearable. Then an idea came to me when I was changing the screen saver image on my computer: I could change my mental screen saver image of Alex! I got myself relaxed, closed my eyes, and let myself daydream about Alex in the months before his accident. In my mind's eye, I scrolled to the day he ran his first marathon, and I zoomed in on my mental picture of Alex joyously crossing the finish line. I concentrated on this image of Alex whenever I was bothered by the morgue flashbacks, and it really helped. After a few weeks, the flashbacks stopped. Now the image of Alex at the finish line is a daily comfort to me."

Intentional dreams, lucid dreams, and daydreams represent other possible grief dream types. Although these three types of dreams are somewhat rare during bereavement, two other types of noncore grief dreams—series dreams and prophetic dreams—are frequently reported by dreamers. Both are explored in the following discussion.

SERIES DREAMS

Some dreams are best understood when grouped together and studied in sequence. Frightening or puzzling dreams are most helpful when they are seen in the context of subsequent dreams. Later dreams often shed light on how to interpret earlier dreams. This progression of meaning is demonstrated by Sam's set of dreams about his deceased wife, Lavinia:

"In the first dream, I saw Lavinia sitting at the kitchen table drinking tea. 'You're alive!' I yelled, shocked, but overjoyed. She just continued to sip her tea and said nothing. In the second dream, Lavinia was dancing, dressed in red. I called to her. Again, she said nothing. But in the final dream, she was about to board an airplane. She turned to me and smiled. She waved good-bye and stepped on the plane. It was only after that third dream that I got it! Lavinia came back to me to say good-bye."

Sam's three dreams of Lavinia are most helpful to him once he is able to understand them in sequence. Sam's first two dreams are frustrating; he calls to his wife, but she does not respond. It is only after the third dream that Sam feels some measure of resolution: he values the dreams as Lavinia's way of saying a gradual good-bye.

Shannon's Dream Series

Often the final dream answers questions raised by earlier dreams. This is particularly true for recurrent traumatic dreams. A poignant example is Shannon's set of dreams following the death of her premature, six-week-old infant nephew, Ethan.

My first dream of Ethan occurred the night before his funeral. I was holding Ethan in the neonatal intensive care unit (NICU) shortly after they unhooked his lifesaving machinery. He was looking up at me and asking me why they were doing this to him. The dream happened several times throughout the night. The only difference was that in each dream, he would look different.

In my second dream of Ethan, I was in an NICU. The babies in the unit were of all sizes, but they were all healthy. Ethan was there, but he didn't look like himself, and he was reassuring me that he was fine and as healthy as the other infants. I was surprised and relieved that the babies were OK and not suffering. This NICU was not the stress-filled, emotional one Ethan was in during his short life, but more like a regular nursery, where healthy babies are cared for. This was the NICU in heaven in my dream.

Symbolic Analysis of Shannon's Dreams

For those readers who have suffered the devastating experience of losing a premature infant, Shannon's story will be tragically familiar. Shannon's first recurring dream is so traumatic that it must be understood in light of the second dream. Initially, the struggling baby, Ethan, in all his different physical sizes, and in his words to Shannon, represents Shannon's struggle to come to grips with the circumstances of Ethan's death in the NICU. This dream asks the question, "Does Ethan really have to die, and is he OK?"

In the second dream, Shannon's struggle shifts to surprise and relief that all the babies are OK, not suffering, and healthy. Now Ethan is reassuring Shannon that he is fine in the "NICU in heaven." We can see how the first dream asks the dreamer's tough questions; the second dream provides a response that is meaningful to the dreamer. Jung termed this the *subjective level* of dream analysis: each feature of a dream series provides a way for the dreamer to work on a serious problem. This is a powerful example of the healing power of a dream series.

Pat's Dream Series

To illustrate another way to work on series dreams, we turn now to Pat's dreams of her beloved brother, Steve, who died unexpectedly of heart failure at age forty-two. This method of dreamwork is complex and involves tracking a recurring image as it changes from dream to dream. As you read Pat's dreams, notice how Steve's appearance changes in sequence: we will demonstrate how these changes provide a key to unlocking potent meaning for Pat.

Two months after Steve passed, I had a dream about him. Everything was white, and Steve stood facing me at the end of this hall dressed in all white, holding white books and folders, with a big smile on his face. When I woke up, I knew I had been with Steve and felt warm and content in his love.

My second dream came about five months after Steve's death. I was standing with Steve and my other brother, Don. Steve looked at his wrist and said, "We have to go. The ball game is going to start in fifteen minutes." Steve was dressed in jeans and T-shirt. I woke up and felt a warm feeling of love.

About seven or eight months after Steve's death, I dreamed I was in some sort of trouble. A voice said not to worry, that my brother was here to help me, and out from behind a partition walked Steve. He was wearing a black suit with a white shirt and black tie. He carried a black briefcase and had a smirkish smile on his face. Again, I woke up with that warm feeling of love.

My fourth and final dream of Steve happened about ten months after he passed. I was standing in the midst of people and up walked Steve, dressed in a brown tweed suit. He came up to me real close with a big smile on his face. I gave him a big hug and kissed him. When I woke up, I could still physically feel that hug and kiss!

Pat adds the following commentary: "In each dream, I remembered the way Steve was dressed, like it was a progression. I want to add here that I started attending a grief counseling group six months after Steve passed. One of our assignments was to write a letter to our loved one. At the end of my letter, I thanked Steve for visiting me in my dreams, and I pray that his visits will never end. My dreams have been a great help to me in my grieving process."

Symbolic Analysis of Pat's Dreams

Pat identifies Steve's appearance as the salient feature of the dream series. She insightfully evaluates the changes in his dress as a *progression*. Let's now analyze the dream symbols, as they offer progressive assistance to Pat's grief process. To simplify this process, we'll amplify one symbol in each dream to gather a cumulative interpretation of the dream set.

In the first dream, the color white is the predominant symbol. We might ask about Pat's personal associations to the color white, then turn to the general or *collective* meanings of the color white. One dream dictionary identifies *white* as awareness, or clearness of mind, whereas another states that the color white signifies hope, light-heartedness, innocence, and the capacity for renewal.

To anchor the meaning of the dream, it is useful to ask a question about the amplified dream symbol, such as this: "How might an awareness of hope, lightheartedness, and the capacity for renewal be helpful to me just now?" Indeed, Pat has indicated that her first dream gave her a loving experience of being "with Steve," which brought hopeful comfort to her in the first months after his death.

In the second dream, Steve is dressed in jeans and T-shirt, ready to go to the ball game. We might generalize that this is the lighthearted Steve, gathering his sister and brother for spirited fun. Jung writes that dreams can bring balance and renewal to the dreamer's waking life: Pat's heavy daytime grief is offset by her dream of a lighthearted Steve, dressed and ready for play.

In the third dream, Steve appears specifically to help Pat, who is in "some sort of trouble." Now Steve is dressed in a black suit and black tie, carrying a black briefcase. His attire can be seen as an image of "getting to work" or "getting down to business." Our symbol research reveals that the color *black* can signify death and the unknown, but it can also symbolize fertile soil, indicating, perhaps, a new ability to understand previously unknown issues.

Moving again from the symbolic meaning to an analytical question, we might ask, "What is the trouble in my life right now, and how can Steve's image help me get down to business and work on this problem?" The "trouble" might be an active issue in Pat's life now, or it might be the ongoing difficulty of grief work. Either way, this third dream offers Pat help in the form of Steve's loving persistence and businesslike focus on the problem at hand.

In Pat's final dream, Steve is dressed in a tweed suit, offering Pat a loving embrace. Webster's (symbol dictionaries don't have tweed as a listing) defines *tweed* as a "rough woolen fabric" that is "informal or suggestive of the outdoors." A rough texture could be remembered by Pat in her dream embrace, and we would ask Pat to use the "feel" of Steve's tweed suit as a memory prompt. This way, she is able to keep Steve's embrace with her whenever she needs it.

A further meaning might be that now Pat can hold on to an inner image of Steve, at all times in all places, in formal and informal moments of waking life, indoors and outdoors, so to speak. Notice that the "feel" of Steve actually survives the initial dream. As already discussed (see Susan's dream in Chapter Four), this lingering physical sensation is not uncommon in grief dreams.

Now we gather the dreams together for serial meaning. We see how in each dream, Steve is *progressively* more *with* Pat as a helpful, inner guide. In the first dream, Steve is the messenger of hope. In the second dream, he is the casually dressed, lighthearted brother of the sibling trio. In the third dream, Steve is more businesslike, ready for deeper work on Pat's "trouble." Finally, in the fourth dream, Steve is palpably present for Pat: his rough tweed suit provides a good grip for Pat's enduring inner embrace of her loving brother.

Toolbox: How to Work on Your Grief Dream Series

With Shannon's dreams of Ethan, we have seen how a pair of dreams can work together to hold and heal raw grief. In addition, we've seen how Pat's dream series signals an attitude of hopeful renewal and offers progressive images of healing guidance. Use the following techniques to work on your grief dreams as a series:

1. In your grief dream journal, use a consistent format to note the following information: the date of the dream; the number of weeks, months, and years since the death of your loved one—for example, *Dream number one:* November 12, 2004; one week after Gram's death.

2. Read and reread your dreams aloud. The process of listening to your dreams as you speak them can shed new light on the details of the dream. And, of course, we continue to emphasize that you share your dreams for perspective and for

comfort. Like Pat, you might join a grief group that will be supportive of your dreamwork.

3. Group your dreams in a sequence that is meaningful to you. For example, you might use all of the dreams you've had within the first six months of your loss. Alternatively, you might choose to focus on the dreams where your loved one appears. As you examine your dream series, track recurring images and themes. Make note of these features. (You might use colored pens, high-lighting, or notations in the margin of your grief dream journal.) Then note the changes in the dreams—physical appearances, ages, behaviors, and scene differences.

4. Now take the feature that is most striking to you and track it through each dream. For example, Pat focuses on her brother's appearance. Make a simple notation with ellipses to show how the feature changes. Pat's notation would look like this:

- Steve in white . . . Steve in jeans . . . Steve in black suit . . . Steve in tweed suit . . .

5. Using your notation, start with the first item and begin researching the main symbol. Symbols are best understood by listing your personal associations and by looking up the word in a dream dictionary. Make a list of your own thoughts under the key word. Then use your dictionaries. We suggest using a regular dictionary as well as a symbol dictionary. Collect the descriptions that ring true for you, personally. Write down the meaningful notations under the key words in your notation. Pat's amplified list might look like this:

- Steve in white . . .
- . . . white is "hope and renewal, lightheartedness"
- Steve in jeans and T-shirt . . .
- . . . jeans and ball game are "fun, lighthearted"

- Steve in suit . . .
- . . . black suit means "business and deeper work on my trouble"
- Steve in tweed . . .
- . . . tweed is a striking texture, grip on memory of Steve's embrace

6. Now, as you study your list, think about the feature symbolically as it changes from dream to dream. What information does it give you? What are you learning about your relationship with your loved one? How are you accepting the loss? Are you sorting through your emotions about your deceased loved one? Are you feeling an internalized sense of being with your loved one through your dreams? Are you learning something valuable about yourself and your life through your dream series? Write these insights in your grief dream journal. They are the gems you have mined from your symbolic work with your dream series.

One of the questions we're most often asked is this: Do grief dreams have prophetic powers? We suspect that America's newfound fascination with psychics and mediums has much to do with this kind of question. Because so many of our dream story contributors and regular Web site visitors (www.griefdreams.com) have inquired about this particular grief dream type, we decided to devote the next several pages to this intriguing topic.

PROPHETIC DREAMS

"I had a dream in which my mother warned me to see a doctor," says Stan. "I'm in pretty good health, so I really didn't take the warning very seriously—that is, until I shared the dream with my wife, who urged me to have a checkup, which I did. I was surprised to learn that my blood pressure was dangerously high. My doctor put me on medication, and he told me it was lucky I came in when I did. I never really believed that our deceased loved ones could talk to us through dreams, much less predict the future, but I guess my mom really is still looking out for me."

Did Stan receive a prophetic warning from his deceased mother, or was his elevated blood pressure just a coincidence?

Strange Coincidences?

"The night before Thanksgiving," says Carin, "I had a dream that my dad was sitting at the dinner table in his usual seat, telling us what he was thankful for. He thanked me for being with him and helping him to pass. He also thanked me for planning his funeral service, giving a eulogy, and for supporting my mother. I didn't tell my mother about the dream because I didn't want to upset her. At Thanksgiving dinner, my mother handed me a card in which she basically thanked me for the very same things Dad thanked me for in the dream."

Although we could easily attribute both Stan and Carin's dreams to mere coincidence, we must open ourselves to the possibility that these dreams are much more. The larger question, of course, is whether dreams can predict future events. And this question brings us back to a similar question asked earlier: Is it possible for us to actually communicate with our loved ones through our dreams (including prophetic dreams)? In Chapter Four, we outlined two views: one view holds that communication (including prophetic messages) through dreams is indeed possible. Many people ascribe to this view and can cite numerous instances to back up their claims.

The other view perceives dreams as a function of the psyche or as windows to the unconscious. Those who hold this view might claim that prophetic dreams are either meaningful coincidences or (as Freud might say) *projections* of the unconscious.

Jung, of course, believed that the unconscious could be revealed in our dreams, but he also placed great value on premonitions and *synchronistic experiences* or *meaningful coincidence*. We could easily classify Stan and Carin's experiences as synchronistic, but we might also view these dreams as projections of the dreamer's unconscious fears, wishes, or anxieties.

For example, perhaps Stan had an intuitive sense that he was ill. His prophetic dream, therefore, could be explained as the work of his personal unconscious acting on his own repressed health concerns. Carin's prophetic dream may be the result of her imagining that her father was grateful to her or *should* have been grateful and that her mother was, in fact, grateful.

After carefully reading the evidence on both sides of this issue, our outlook encompasses all viewpoints. As we have already pointed out, the study of dreams, particularly the study of grief dreams, is a work in progress, and there's really no definitive answer to the question concerning the veracity of prophetic dreams. In truth, having a definitive answer one way or the other is of secondary importance, because our focus remains steadfastly on the *meaning the dream has for the dreamer*.

What Do We Know About Prophetic Dreams?

First, all prophetic dreams are also message dreams. Ellen's dream (in Chapter Four) of her grandmother, who appears in a dream to offer a prophetic message about Ellen's mother, is an example of a prophetic message dream. Second, prophetic dreams are dreams in which the dreamer is somehow made aware of an event before it actually occurs. (See Marcus's dream later in the chapter.) Third, although we do not fully understand this phenomenon, we *do* know that prophetic (or *precognitive*) dreams have been recorded throughout history by nearly every major civilization. Many ancient cultures believed that dreams contained omens for the future, and often, the gods would convey prophetic messages through dreams.

The Bible is filled with prophetic dream stories—ranging from the soldier's dream of Gideon's victory over the Midianites in the book of Judges to the Gospel of Matthew's chilling description of the foreboding dream of Pilate's wife (which she shared with her husband but was ignored): "Have nothing to do with that innocent man [Jesus], for today I have suffered a great deal because of a dream about him" (27:19). The litmus test of a prophetic dream, of course, is whether the prophecy actually comes to fruition.

Finally, even today, a great number of perfectly rational people all over the world believe it is possible for our loved ones to appear in dreams with messages, warnings, and even predictions of future events. Some cite the experience of *déjà vu*—the feeling that we have been in a certain place or have experienced a certain event before—as evidence of prophetic dreams. That is, we had a similar experience in a dream, so what *appears* to be a new place, event, or experience, is actually familiar to us because we have already "been there" in a dream.

Prophetic Dreams and the Paranormal

Those who study prophetic dreaming usually classify these dreams as an aspect of extra sensory perception, or ESP. This classification, of course, means that prophetic dreams are usually considered part of the paranormal experience, a designation some may find off-putting. "I don't believe in psychics or mediums or any of that paranormal stuff," says Vincent. "All I know is that for the past nine years, my wife has occasionally appeared to me in dreams to warn me about certain people who might not have my best interest at heart or to remind me of certain things." Although Vincent's position reflects the viewpoint of many dreamers, others are inclined to disagree.

"I dreamed of my brother-in-law's death over a year before it happened," says Lisa. "The dream scared me as I am very prophetic and can predict major world events as well as close events." Lisa has learned to trust the information conveyed to her through her dreams because, on more than one occasion, her dreams warned her of impending events that actually happened.

Although some may question Lisa's ability to actually predict local and world events, Jung, himself, describes a few prophetic dreams of his own in his autobiography. In fact, his own dreams and visions helped him to formulate his theories concerning the personal and the collective unconscious. (For more on Jung's theories on the personal and collective unconscious, review Chapter Two and the Reader Resources section.)

Opportunities for Change

One of the most interesting aspects of prophetic dreams is that they offer the dreamer the opportunity to potentially change or modify the outcome of certain events. For instance, irrespective of the true nature of Stan's prophetic dream (that is, whether Stan's dream was initiated by his mother or came from deep within Stan himself), because of his dream, he consulted a physician, who confirmed his hypertension and prescribed lifesaving medication, thereby avoiding a potentially dangerous health crisis.

"My aunt came to me in a dream," says Marcus. "She warned me not to go to a certain bar. In the dream, she said: 'Stay away from Reggie's. Somebody's going to get hurt there.' The dream scared me enough to keep away from Reggie's for a couple of weeks. Good thing, too, because a week after the dream, I heard on the news that there was a fight at the bar and an innocent bystander was shot and killed. Who knows? That bystander could have been me, and my aunt seemed to know it."

Again, we could either attribute Marcus's dream to coincidence or perhaps to Marcus's own intuitive sense that Reggie's was a dangerous place. It's clear, however, that both Stan and Marcus view their dreams as prophetic, lifesaving gifts from deceased loved ones. And based on the positive outcome of both dreams, it really doesn't matter whether or not this view is "correct."

Dream Divination

Dream divination, like prophetic dreaming, refers to the ability of the dreamer to obtain information about the future through dreams. The difference, however, is that in the case of dream divination, the dreamer relies on someone else to interpret the prophetic message in the dream—a so-called dream diviner or seer. The word *divination* comes from the root word *deus*, meaning "god," or *divus*, meaning "pertaining to god." The connotation, then, is that certain dream messages may be supernatural or even divine in origin.

The practice of dream divination is well documented in ancient cultures, including the Babylonians, Greeks, Romans, Egyptians, and Israelites. The biblical tale of Joseph and his brothers, for example, features Joseph in the role of dream diviner for the pharaoh, who has a series of disturbing dreams. Although Pharaoh is perplexed concerning the meaning of his dreams, Joseph interprets the dreams as prophecies concerning a future famine (which comes true).

Although dream divination is closely related to prophetic dreaming, divinatory dreams are usually more symbolic in nature. For instance, a prophetic dream might feature your deceased husband urging you to have the wiring in your house inspected in order to prevent a fire. In a divinatory dream, you might simply see a home on fire.

In many ways, modern dream divination is similar to dream sharing. That is, sometimes the message of the dream is unclear to the dreamer until it is shared with someone else. "In my dream," says Alicia, "my mother was walking through an art gallery and pointing to the various paintings and making unpleasant faces. I'm a college student, and I just declared art as my major. I thought the dream might be Mom's way of voicing her disapproval of my decision to major in art. But when I told my pastor about the dream, she smiled and said, 'Perhaps your mother was trying to tell you that your work surpasses the work of other, more accomplished artists.' It wasn't until three weeks later, when I was awarded a blue ribbon for one of my paintings during a local art competition, that I realized my pastor was right. I definitely think Mom already knew I would win. Now I know I made the right decision with regard to my college major."

Toolbox: How Prophetic Dreams Can Help You

Although prophetic grief dreams can sometimes be unsettling, most dreamers tend to view these rare and special dreams as helpful. Prophetic grief dreams can help you in the following ways.

1. *Maintaining connections*. One of the most difficult aspects of any grief experience is the pain of separation. Prophetic dreams remind us that our loved ones are still very much connected to us, watching over us, and helping to keep us out of harm's way. "I feel like Mom is still looking out for me." "My husband is still helping me make important decisions."

2. *Getting practical help*. Many prophetic dreams are utilitarian in nature. For example, Stan's dream prompted him to seek medical attention for an undiagnosed health problem, and the warning from Marcus's aunt kept him out of danger.

3. *Visualizing creative new possibilities*. Sometimes prophetic messages can help us step out of the insular world of grief and open us up to new possibilities. These possibilities may be as simple as Carin's affirmation: "Dad appreciates what I did for him." Alternatively, they may be more complex, as in Alicia's dream of her mother, predicting the outcome of an art competition (which, to Alicia, demonstrates her mother's support of her decision to major in art and thus allows Alicia to move forward with her life).

4. *Clarifying feelings*. Finally, prophetic dreams help us understand how we're really feeling, on a deeper level that may not be obvious to us in our daily consciousness.

PSYCHICS AND MEDIUMS

Throughout history, people have reported a wide range of paranormal experiences, ranging from *déjà vu* to spiritual visitations. The ancients often enlisted the help of specialized seers to conjure up the spirits of the deceased (who appeared both in dreams and in waking states) to offer help or guidance in urgent matters. The Bible, for example, tells the story of King Saul, who first forbids the use of mediums but then breaks his own law and calls upon the Witch of Endor to conjure up the spirit of the deceased prophet Samuel for guidance in an upcoming battle. Even though the Bible clearly forbids the use of mediums, the practice was nonetheless widespread and regarded as a legitimate means of communication with the deceased.

Today, more than ever before, many bereaved people turn to psychics and mediums to help them decipher their dreams or to contact deceased loved ones. But just what do we mean when we speak of psychics and mediums? Although the terms *psychic* and *medium* are often used interchangeably, there are some subtle differences between the two.

A psychic is a person who claims to have the ability to connect with another's soul. By reading an individual's *aura* (or energy field), the psychic can learn about the person's past, present, and future. A medium, in contrast, claims to receive information from the deceased and then transmits this information to loved ones. Sometimes this information can be overt; more often though, it comes in the form of feelings or images. Some mediums claim to actually hear, taste, or smell aspects of messages. Essentially, a medium serves as a sort of conduit from the world beyond to the earthly realm. Most agree that mediums are also psychics, but not all psychics are mediums. Both psychics and mediums claim to have the ability to interpret dreams and to affirm whether a particular dream is prophetic in nature.

Opinions are divided concerning the legitimacy of modern psychics and mediums, but there is no denying the fact that there has been a renewed interest in the paranormal during the last several years. Witness the popularity of television programs such as *Crossing Over* with John Edward and *Beyond* with James Van Praagh. Both shows feature mediums who profess an ability to connect select audience members with deceased loved ones "on the other side." Although there is much debate concerning the veracity of these programs, faithful viewers, as well as those who have been "read" by Edward or Van Praagh, usually report feelings of great comfort and consolation as a result of their reading.

"My father died of cancer several months ago," says Carin (whom we met earlier). "Since he's been gone, my mother and I have had several grief dreams about him. We've also had contact with him through a medium, who is a friend of mine, and we've received many comforting messages from him, telling us that he's still with us and watching over us. While he was alive, my father and I went to the medium twice for spiritual healings. Although his body was not healed, I truly believe that our experience with her educated us and healed our spirits so that we were able to endure the huge loss of such a wonderful man."

Like Carin, millions of people all over the world have engaged the help of psychics or mediums to help them contact their deceased loved ones either through dreams or through *awake readings*. Some have turned to psychics and mediums for help in interpreting their dreams.

"My boyfriend, Trey (who was killed in a boating accident), appeared in my dream with an armful of pink roses," says Lani. "I really didn't know what the dream meant until I heard John Edward say on his show that pink roses symbolize great love. This made me feel really happy because now I know that Trey was trying to tell me he still loves me."

Psychic Sylvia Browne's best-selling book on dreams asserts that our dreams can influence our health, our relationships, and even our future. Browne also says that it is possible to receive prophetic messages from our departed loved ones. In fact, she devotes an entire chapter in her book (*Sylvia Browne's Book of Dreams*) to prophetic dreams. Browne says that all prophetic dreams have two things in common: they are always in color, and they follow a logical sequence (as opposed to the often random nature of most dreams). We should note that we don't necessarily agree with Browne's assertions concerning the two common elements of prophetic dreams; indeed, we've received many prophetic dreams that lack both of Browne's common elements. Conversely, some dreamers have reported to us that their prophetic dreams are both in color and follow a logical sequence.

In any case, Browne cautions dreamers who might act on the prophetic messages conveyed in dreams. She says that most prophetic messages are too vague and incomplete to be of any real help to the dreamer. This is not to say that she does not value the importance of prophetic dreams, only that dreamers should carefully evaluate the messages before acting on them.

Toolbox: Finding a Psychic or Medium to Help You with Your Grief Dreams

The focus of this Toolbox is how to avoid some of the common pitfalls when engaging the services of a psychic or medium. Although there are compelling arguments for and against the use of psychics and mediums, our basic position is simple: if you feel that a psychic or medium is helpful to you in your grief, then by all means, continue to work with that person. If you are considering contacting a psychic or medium to help you better understand the prophetic messages in your grief dreams (or for general grief support), please consider the following general suggestions:

1. Do your homework. Research a particular psychic or medium's background, and if possible, go with a recommendation

from someone who has been satisfied with a particular psychic or medium's work.

2. Interview several psychics or mediums and get a feel for costs. In general, avoid those who charge very little or those who charge too much. Settle on a price before your visit. Never agree to give large sums of money up front.

3. Stay away from psychic hot lines; many are costly and unreliable.

4. Make sure that your psychic or medium has experience in dreamwork. Make a list of questions, and be sure he or she answers all of your questions to your satisfaction.

5. Use your own good common sense. If something doesn't feel right about the reading, trust your instincts and leave immediately.

The brief glimpse of other grief dream types presented in this chapter illustrates the diverse possibilities of our dreams. In reviewing many of the dream stories in this book, you may find certain common *dream themes* beginning to emerge. For example, many dreams feature a deceased loved one who does not speak in the dream; often the dreamer is frustrated by this. One of the most prevalent grief dream themes has to do with religious symbols or images. Because this theme is such a dominant one in grief dreams, and because many mourners have general questions about faith in the context of loss, we felt that a chapter devoted to these issues was in order. Let us now turn to Chapter Eight to explore Faith and Grief Dreams.

8

Faith and Grief Dreams

God is greater than any mortal.
Why do you contend against him,
saying, "He will answer none of
my words?"
For God speaks in one way,
and in two, though people do
not perceive it.
In a dream, in a vision of the
night,
When deep sleep falls on
mortals,
While they slumber on their
beds,
Then he opens their ears.

Job

After my baby died," says Charlotte, "I wanted to die, too. Each night, I would pray to God to take me so that I could be with my daughter. One night, about three weeks after Victoria's death, I saw her in a dream. She was laying in a beautiful, white bassinet, and I somehow knew she was in heaven. She looked happy and very peaceful. I looked away briefly, and when I looked back, there was a beautiful angel, surrounded in an aura of bright light, standing beside her bassinet. The angel told me, 'Victoria is not very far away. When you think of her, she will be with you.' I woke up, and for the first time since my baby's death, I felt a small glimmer of hope. Even now, twenty years later, this dream brings me great comfort."

Like Charlotte, many mourners (even those who do not describe themselves as particularly religious) report grief dreams filled with religious images. These images may be obvious, as in Charlotte's heavenly dream, or they may appear in a more understated form, as in Jason's dream:

"My dad died of throat cancer after several grueling operations that left him disfigured. On the first anniversary of his passing, I had a dream about him. He was dressed all in white and looked radiant—glowing, actually. Although the setting of the dream was in his hospital room, I had the feeling that Dad was trying to tell me that he was OK now. I felt really happy when I woke up, and the dream helped me feel less angry about the way God allowed him to suffer, especially at the end."

Jason, like Charlotte, is consoled by his beautiful, deeply spiritual dream. You may have already observed that many of the grief dreams presented in this book are also quite spiritual in nature. (Recall, for example, Valerie's reassurance dream in Chapter Five.) Many believe that all grief dreams are by their very nature spiritual, but there are some dreams that are clearly more overtly religious than others. Before we explore the religious images and symbols commonly found in grief dreams, let us first discuss faith (or the lack thereof) within the general context of grief.

GRIEF AND FAITH

As children, many of us are taught three basic things about God: God is all-loving, all-knowing, and all-powerful. Those who accept these assertions move through life secure in the knowledge that God loves them and will protect them from harm. In the face of grief, however, any reasonably intelligent person might logically wonder about this: if God is a God of knowledge, power, and love, how could God allow this to happen?

The Question of Theodicy

Questions about God, faith, and religion are nearly universal grief reactions. In fact, these questions are so commonplace that pastoral counselors often call them the *questions of theodicy*. When referred to in this way, *theodicy* has to do with the apparent disparity between the existence of a God who supposedly loves us yet still permits suffering and grief to enter our lives.

Throughout history, mystics, sages, teachers, and clergy of every kind have wrestled with the theodicy issue, and many thoughtful responses have been put forth in an effort to reconcile an all-loving, all-knowing, and all-powerful God alongside the reality of suffering. Such responses include the following:

- Perhaps our suffering is God's way of teaching us (or others) some valuable lesson.

- Everything happens for a reason, even if that reason is unclear to us.

- Maybe our suffering has a higher purpose, one that is hidden from us (a "mystery").

- Suffering is a punishment for our sins.

- God is a detached deity who can't be bothered with day-to-day life here on Earth.

Clearly, none of these reasons is particularly appealing, and none seem to address the obvious: if God really loved us, God would not intentionally cause us to suffer, for any reason. Of course, this statement centers on the premise that God is somehow the cause of our suffering—or at the very least is able to stop it. Many theologians and clergy feel that the basic premise itself is in error. In fact, many dismiss the notion that God purposely inflicts pain and grief on us and instead speak of suffering as a natural consequence of living in a less-than-perfect world. Others maintain that God is limited because of the basic law of free will. (If God intervened in human affairs, this would disrupt the natural freedom of the universe.)

Even though some of these responses are helpful and certainly more consoling than simply ascribing to the philosophy that "everything happens for a reason" (after all, what possible "reason" is worth the sacrifice of even one precious life?), perhaps there is yet another alternative. Maybe we can simply learn to live with the question. Sometimes, when there are no satisfying answers, living with the question is the best we can do.

Ways Faith Can Help You in Your Grief

Many mourners find strength and comfort in their religious affiliations and instinctively turn to the familiar rituals and religious practices that have sustained them in the past. Even those who describe themselves as "marginally religious" often feel deep consolation in returning to their old childhood faith practices. "I'm not a religious person at all," says Ken. "I go with my wife to church services on Christmas and Easter, but that's about it. Ever since my father died, though, I've found that going to church more often has helped me in my grief. I've learned that there is comfort in prayer, and other church members seem to genuinely care about me. And to be honest, the older I get, the more I think about God, heaven, and the meaning of life. This particular church has helped me to grapple with some of the issues I have surrounding all three."

Ken not only feels a renewal of faith in light of his loss but also mentions a very important but sometimes overlooked aspect of faith: community support. Belonging to a particular congregation can help connect us with others who have experienced the death of a loved one, both within our contemporary faith community and through the stories found in religious scriptures, like the Bible. These connections affirm our loss and help us feel less isolated in our suffering.

"If it weren't for the support of my rabbi and temple community," says Emily, "I never would have made it through my husband's illness and death. So many people reached out to me and my son with caring and loving gestures. The cards, meals, and prayers meant more to us than words could ever describe."

Herman Melville observed that humans are connected by a thousand fibers. At a time when they are feeling particularly isolated and vulnerable, most grieving people certainly need such connections. Mourners, like Emily and Ken, who have built-in support systems through their local place of worship, are indeed fortunate. Although some congregations are slow to recognize the unique needs of bereaved members, many offer specialized grief support. Some ministers, priests, rabbis, and other clergy may even have specialized training in pastoral or grief counseling.

"I must say that going to church and living a faithful life is something new for me," says Jayme. "We had religion forced down our throats as kids, and frankly, I couldn't wait to escape to college where I promptly declared myself an agnostic. When my mother died, I hadn't been to church in almost twenty years. I took Mom's death the hardest of the three kids, and when counseling and antidepressants failed, my brother and his wife dragged me to their church. 'Just try if for a month,' they pleaded. I figured I had nothing to lose. I can't begin to describe how this small church has helped me—both in my grief and more generally, in my life. The people are kind and understanding, and for the first time, I finally understand what real faith is all about."

Aside from the congregational aspects of religion, there are the teachings of a particular faith community. Religions attempt to explore and give meaning to the mysteries of life, including the pain and separation of death.

Many religions offer the hope of eternal life, either in another realm (heaven or paradise) or through rebirth into this world. Many of the dreamers who have shared their dream stories with us in this book have found great consolation in this belief. Recall, for example, the final words of Arlene's back story, "My faith has strengthened because I know that he [her brother, Rich] is with God."

Unbelievers

Many mourners report that their ongoing faith practices have enabled them to endure the pain of grief, but it's also not unusual for bereaved people (like Ken and Jayme) to feel a revival of faith or to experience the joy of true faith for the first time. But what about those who feel that their faith has been badly shaken (or completely abandoned) by their loss? And what can be said of those who, by choice or circumstance, do not believe in a higher power or eschew religious beliefs altogether?

Before we discuss those who have experienced a lapse or loss of faith during bereavement, let's first say a few words about "unbelievers." Very generally speaking, unbelievers usually identify themselves as either agnostic (those who feel it's impossible to know if God exists) or atheist (those who deny the existence of a God). Assuming a person is comfortable with his or her identity as either an agnostic or an atheist, it would be a mistake to assume that nonbelievers are at a disadvantage when it comes to coping with grief.

"My mother keeps telling me that the reason I've had such a difficult time dealing with my wife's death is because I don't have a personal relationship with God," says Greg. "But she's wrong. I miss Carol and I feel cheated out of the chance to grow old with her. I loved her deeply, and that's why all of this is so difficult. I respect my mother as a person of faith; I just wish she respected my choice to see things differently."

Greg's statement captures the universal pain of all grief, regardless of religious orientation. Indeed, much of grief is missing and yearning for the one we love. Some may argue that believers are consoled and comforted by their brothers and sisters in faith and that they are able to enjoy the healing presence of God in a way that unbelievers cannot. Nonbelievers are likely to counter with the assertion that they receive consolation from their own community of friends, family, and colleagues. As for a healing presence, many nonbelievers find such a presence in other ways—in nature, art, and music, just to name a few.

"As a professional musician, I have always believed in music. For me, music has a sacredness about it that I think others find in religion," says Micah. "I also like to believe that as long as I'm alive, my sister will live on through me. And when I have children, she will live on in them. In this way, Judith is eternal."

Micah reminds us that *faith* comes in many forms, and our beloved continues on in our near and dear ones; in stories, photographs, memories, and, of course, in our dreams.

How Grief Challenges Faith

Following the death of his wife, C. S. Lewis, a man known for his deep faith, wrote the following in his grief journal:

> Talk to me about the truth of religion and I'll listen gladly. Talk to me about the duty of religion and I'll listen submissively. But don't come talking to me about the consolations of religion or I shall suspect that you don't understand [A *Grief Observed*, p. 28].

Many mourners—even those who have formerly expressed an abiding faith—resonate with Lewis's words. But why—at a time when faith *should* comfort and sustain us—does it sometimes prove to be elusive? As we've already pointed out, grief brings with it a flood of feelings and emotions, many of which we've never experienced before. Some of these feelings are transient—like shock and denial—whereas others reflect real changes in our perspective, such as Alison's "emerging sense of interior freedom and differentiation" following her sister's death (see Chapter Three).

In early grief, it's often difficult to distinguish between transient grief responses and real changes in perspective. This distinction is an important one because, quite often, what previously faithful mourners perceive as a permanent loss of faith may instead be a temporary grief response.

"I've gone to church all my life," says Jill. "I believed that if I lived my life according to God's laws and the church, he would protect me and my family. However, when my five-year-old daughter died suddenly from a brain hemorrhage, I lost my faith. I felt betrayed by God and very angry. How could God allow such a terrible thing to happen to Molly and to us?

"My pastor tried to convince me that Molly's death was part of 'God's mysterious plan.' What kind of a 'plan' involves the senseless death of a child? I left the church, feeling even more broken and distraught. After about a year, when my ten-year marriage was crumbling, I went to grief counseling. My new pastoral counselor helped me to see how anger prevented me from turning to God for comfort. I realized that I still loved God, despite the negative feelings I had about my church and pastor. Although I won't be returning to my old church—or any other church, for that matter—I no longer hold God responsible for Molly's death. Molly died because of a brain defect, not because of some divine plan. I like to think that God feels as badly about all of this as I do."

Jill's initial reactions—betrayal and anger directed at God—are common, but temporary, grief reactions and do not represent a true change in perspective. Over time, and with the help of a caring counselor, Jill realizes that her love for God is enduring. There does seem to be a change in Jill's perspective regarding her pastor and church, but in time, there is a chance that Jill may learn to forgive her pastor and resume attending the church she once loved.

Most grief counselors recommend that mourners refrain from making any major life decisions (moving, divorce, changing jobs) for at least a year or more following the death of a loved one. The reason for this is that when we're grieving, we see the world through tear-filled eyes—which sometimes clouds our judgment. Recall, for example, how dreamers, like Janet (in Chapter Three) and Nadine (in Chapter Six), who initially viewed certain dreams as painful or traumatic, later came to recognize the healing aspects of their dreams. So it is in bereavement: time offers healing and perspective.

Toolbox: Holding On to Faith During Bereavement

Death often causes many of us to ask difficult questions about the meaning of life, our role in the world, and the nature of God. Attempts by others to "make sense" of our loss often ring hollow. And we feel yet another loss in the offing: our faith.

Obviously, if your faith has grown stronger or has not been challenged by your loss—or if you consider yourself a nonbeliever—then this Toolbox is not for you. Rather, this Toolbox is for the vast majority of mourners who are currently struggling with their faith following the death of a loved one.

1. Recognize questioning as normal. Grieving people throughout the ages have looked to the heavens and asked, "Why?" Questions during grief are as commonplace as tears. Remember that God can handle your questions. In fact, God is there in the questioning. Share your questions about God, faith, and religion with your clergyperson, therapist or pastoral counselor, grief partner, trusted friend or family member, avoiding those individuals who might chastise you for asking such questions.

2. Accept your feelings. We're often taught to accept others as they are, but we're usually not very good at applying this concept to ourselves. There are no right or wrong ways to grieve, and you do not need to rationalize or apologize for any of the feelings associated with grief—even negative feelings directed at God. Feelings are not a choice; you feel how you feel, period. Accept your feelings of loss, whatever they may be, and recognize them as part of a normal grief response. Repeat this simple affirmation whenever you feel the need:

"I've just lost my loved one, and I'm entitled to the feelings of grief."

3. Resist the urge to abandon your current religious affiliation. Sometimes mourners misinterpret a temporary aversion to religious services (a common grief response) as a rejection of their religion altogether. You are likely to experience some changes in religious attitudes following the death of a loved one, but only the passage of time will enable you to discern whether these changes warrant a radical shift in religious perspective and affiliation. Wait at least one year before making any permanent changes in this regard.

4. Pray. Set aside time specifically for prayer. Find a quiet, comfortable place, free from distractions, and pray *as if* you believe God is actually listening. Assuming such an attitude is important; otherwise, this will be an exercise in futility. Both theologians and psychologists have written extensively on the transformative aspects of prayer, so there's definitely something to it! Think of prayer as an ongoing dialogue with God, and try to focus on one or two things rather than laying out a complete laundry list in one sitting. A specific prayer for patience in dealing with a husband who seems not to understand your grief can be more helpful than asking God to help you deal with all those who have failed to acknowledge your loss.

Now that you have some understanding of the connection between faith and grief, let's explore the ways in which these connections are present in our grief dreams.

RELIGIOUS IMAGES IN GRIEF DREAMS

In many ways, all grief dreams are sacred. We might even go so far as to say that there's a sense of *holiness* associated with our dreams of deceased loved ones. The word *holy* is often used to describe a person, place, or thing that has achieved some status worthy of veneration. But this definition does not reflect the true meaning of the word. The biblical understanding of holy is "other." God is holy, other, unlike us, incomprehensible. And certainly our grief dreams are unlike any other dreams we've ever had; they, too, in many ways, are radically "other."

Those who study the connections between faith and dreams hold that our creator has endowed us with the natural capacity to dream. Although this inborn capability enables us to creatively envision all sorts of new possibilities, it is our grief dreams, in particular, that represent our innate ability to help ourselves better cope with our loss.

Dreams as Answers to Doubts

As we've already pointed out, grief often results in a struggle to make sense of our loss within the context of faith. Such struggles are often carried over to our dreams. "I have always believed in an afterlife," says Colin, "but after my cousin died, I started to wonder if maybe I was just deluding myself; maybe there's nothing at all, outside of this life. One night, before I fell asleep, I was wishing that there were a way for me to know for sure that Ian was in heaven. That night, I had a dream in which Ian, dressed all in white, came to me and told me that he was with God and that the roads really were paved in gold. I woke up right after the dream and wrote it down. When I told my family about the dream, we all felt comforted by it, especially my aunt."

Colin expresses a common wish: If we could only know "for sure" that our loved ones continue to exist in a peaceful realm beyond this earthly one, then the pain of separation would be a bit more bearable. Of course, the majority of Americans (a recent Harris Poll states 82 percent) profess a belief in heaven, but in the face of grief, even deeply held religious beliefs are sometimes questioned.

We've already discussed the notion that dreams are often wish fulfillments, and in this case, Colin certainly receives his wish. In addition, Colin's grief dream serves as an excellent example of how dreams can help us cope with doubt.

"Several weeks after my beloved cat, Patches, died," says Seera, "an angel came to me in a dream. She told me that my time with Patches was over in this lifetime but that our souls would be together again someday." Seera's dream comforts her and reassures her that she will be reunited with Patches in heaven. "For anyone who has ever doubted whether or not animals have souls," says Seera, "this dream helped me believe they do!"

The Religious Language of Dreams

Of course, by now, you're already aware that dreams have their own language, and you're probably becoming fairly well versed in being able to decipher the unique language of your own grief dreams. The religious language of grief dreams resembles the symbolic language of all dreams. Sometimes this language is clear and easily identified by the dreamer; but often the religious symbols are missed, and thus the helpful aspects of the dream might be lost.

Michelle, who admits having a few "issues" with her faith following the death of her boyfriend, William, described a dream in which she climbed a hill. Notice that this dream does not seem to have any overt religious symbols (there are no angels, no white-clad loved ones, no aura of light), but the dream is nonetheless profoundly spiritual:

"It was a beautiful day; the sun was shining and I was out hiking with William. I knew he was dead, but we were having such a marvelous time, I didn't want to mention it. We reached a rather tall, grassy hill, and suddenly William appeared at the top of the hill while I was still at the bottom. I started to cry, and he told me that I'd have to climb the hill if I wanted to be where he was. So I struggled up the hill to reach William. I had a hard time breathing, and I knew the air was clear and clean at the top of the hill. When I finally reached the top, the air was fresh, the sun was bright, and William was there. I woke up from the dream and for the first time since William died said a prayer of thanks to God."

Even though Michelle's dream lacks many of the symbols typically associated with faith, religion, or spirituality, her dream is actually very much a reflection of her faith issues. If we consult a dream dictionary to help us decipher some of the symbols in her dream, we discover that *green grass* often symbolizes new growth or change; *climbing* can mean moving beyond something, working out a problem, or the dreamer's ability to see a new perspective; and a *sunny hillside* is described as a sense of heaven. All of these symbols reflect Michelle's life, as she works through both her grief and her struggles with her faith. This dream, then, is deeply spiritual and holds great meaning for Michelle, so much so that she offers a prayer of thanksgiving upon waking.

Toolbox: How to Create a Healing Affirmation from Your Grief Dreams

The focus of this Toolbox is to help you incorporate the religious images in your grief dreams to create a healing affirmation of comfort.

1. Review your dream journal and note all dreams with religious images. Make a list of each religious image, including less-obvious images, such as Michelle's green, sunny hillside. If you're uncertain regarding the spiritual connections of a particular image, consult one or more dream dictionaries to clarify. If you've had only one dream of this type, that's fine; just list the images from that dream.

2. Next to each religious dream image, write an association to your situation. If you cannot think of an association, then write one or two words that help clarify the image, using a dream dictionary, and leave it at that. You might choose to do

both (write a clarifying description from a dream dictionary *and* an association to you). So using Michelle's dream, her list might look something like this:

- I am climbing . . . I am climbing toward heaven where William is.
- Green . . . new growth . . . *I am growing spiritually.*
- Sunny hillside . . . a sense of heaven.

3. After you complete your list, use the list as an outline for the creation of a special dream affirmation. The purpose of the affirmation is threefold: to help you utilize the religious images in your dreams for comfort and healing beyond the original dream or dreams, to help soothe you during times of spiritual questioning, to create something of lasting beauty that both honors your dream and invokes your loved one.

4. This is *your* special affirmation. It can be short or long; it may rhyme or be in free verse. Before creating your affirmation, reread all dreams containing religious images and note the important details of each dream that you might want to include as part of your affirmation. Again, using Michelle's list and her dream story, her affirmation might be something like the following:

- In my sorrow, I can still recognize many blessings: the green grass, fresh air, sunny hillsides, and most of all, the love I share with William. I know that God will help me as I struggle with my faith and my grief.

5. You may use your affirmation at any time for comfort or to recapture the sacred feeling of your religious image dream.

We would like to conclude this chapter with one of the most in-depth and consoling dreams we received. The author of this dream is Jan, a bereaved parent, first introduced in Chapter Five (see Jan's dream of Beau). The following is Jan's detailed description of her dream visit with Beau in his afterlife existence. As you read Jan's dream story, you will no doubt recognize many of the distinctive characteristics typically associated with grief dreams, including certain dream symbols that by now may seem familiar to you.

We ask that you settle yourself in a quiet place and read Jan's moving and profoundly spiritual dream of Beau. Our wish is that you will be as consoled by this dream as we were.

REUNION WITH BEAU

Jan begins by telling us: "I had this dream of Beau shortly before our first Christmas without him. I went through the motions of preparing for the holiday but felt that I simply could no longer cope; all I wanted to do was to curl up in bed and die.

"One afternoon, while driving home from work, I began to pray. As a Christian, I turned to the mother of Jesus. I figured that since she, too, was a mother who had tragically lost a son, she would naturally understand my pain and heartache. I told her that I was very desperate and that if I could only know for sure that my son was happy where he was—and not missing us terribly—it would help me so much. A few days later, I received the following dream."

My husband and I, along with our two daughters, Ashley and Amanda, ages twelve and thirteen, had taken a trip to a foreign country, where no one spoke English. The day was bleak and dreary. We were on a seashore and hundreds of people were milling about. We found someone who was able to tell us that a person of great importance had died, and the people on the shore had gathered to bid him farewell. The burial custom in this place was to place the body on a small boat and send it out to sea; when it disappeared over the horizon, it meant that the person had crossed to the other side.

I thought to myself, "I would love to travel on that boat to get a glimpse of the other side." With that thought, I suddenly found myself gliding over the water, far out into the ocean. My husband was with me, but our daughters remained on the shore.

The dreary, overcast day seemed to be clearing, and I could see sunlight and an island ahead. All at once, the sunlight was so bright, I thought the air around me would shatter. The colors of everything were so beautiful; they were the brightest colors I had ever seen. People were strolling about everywhere and everything seemed calm and serene. A great feeling of peace and joy surrounded me.

A pier jutted out into the ocean, and on the end of the pier sat my son. He had one leg up with his arm resting on it and the other leg dangling in the water. He was wearing his favorite Nike swimming trunks, and he looked tanned, alive, and well. I wanted to jump for joy. I said to my husband, "Look how tan he's gotten!" My husband felt that he was not tan, but glowing. Our son smiled the most radiant smile I've ever seen and said, "Hi." I told him how well he looked and how glad I was to see him.

Beau looked at me and asked, "Where's Ashley and Amanda?" I told him that they had chosen not to come but were waiting back on the shore for us. He said, "They're not dealing with this too well, are they?" I told him that no, they weren't; they missed him very much.

At this point, sadly, I woke up, startled by the sound of a pan being dropped in the kitchen. I awoke with such joy, and for the first time since my son's death, I could truly say that I knew he was OK. This dream not only carried me through that first Christmas, but it continues to carry me through the dark hours of grief. It has been a long journey through grief for our family. Sometimes we walked, often we stumbled, and sometimes we just had to sit down and rest. And now, when a sad memory or thought takes me by surprise, I try to put myself back in that spot on the ocean by the pier, and I feel all the love and peace that radiated from my son, and I remember . . .

9

How Grief Dreams Help Heal Us

Hope is a waking dream.

Aristotle

In these pages, a montage of dreams has created a vivid documentary of the healing power of grief dreams. To conclude, we return to our original line of inquiry to focus our meaning: How do we understand our dreams? And how do these dream interpretations help heal us? What exactly do we mean by *healing*? How do grieving dreamers explain the healing value of their dreams? And finally, how can health care professionals help?

It is fitting that the voices of our dream contributors, having filled these pages, will conclude this book. But first, let's review our methods in light of your new understanding of grief dreams and define our terms.

METHODS OF DREAM INTERPRETATION

Consider the following observation made by Jung:

> When we consider the infinite variety of dreams, it is difficult to conceive that there could ever be a method or a technical procedure which would lead to an infallible

result. It is, indeed, a good thing . . . for otherwise [we would] lose precisely that virtue which makes dreams so valuable for therapeutic purposes—their ability to offer new points of view [*Collected Works of* C. G. *Jung*, Volume 10, p. 150].

Jung's words remind us that the dreams considered in these pages—and indeed all dreams—elude a single method of interpretation. The very fact that dreams offer new points of view, unrestricted by a particular technique, is the key to their therapeutic value. Similarly, the methods used here for dream amplification and commentary are variably focused to offer dreamers a wide-angle range of viewpoints. To this effect, a broad sample of psychological perspectives has been given, from Freudian *wish fulfillment* and *unconscious projection* to Jungian *synchronicity* and *individuation*. It is our hope that every dreamer can discover personal meaning in these pages. This self-discovery is part of the journey of grief that brings healing.

THE NATURE OF HEALING

We use the word easily, but what exactly do we mean by healing? *To heal* has several dictionary definitions:

- To make sorrow less painful

- To be repaired and restored

- To settle and restore harmony

- To cause a person to become healthy and whole

When we refer back to Chapter Two, we see how these four definitions correspond to the four ways that dreams help us grieve. Let us count the ways.

Grief Dreams Make Sorrow Less Painful by Absorbing Shock

To make sorrow less painful, our first definition of healing, can be read as a sensitive description of the shock-absorbing effect of grief dreams. Chapter Two describes how early grief dreams help survivors digest the shocking pain of death. Most of the dreams presented in this book illustrate that during sleep, sorrow is mediated by images that bring gradual adjustment and titration of pain.

Constance, for example, describes the excruciating pain of losing her seventeen-year-old daughter, Sarah, after a seven-year battle with cancer. In her series of eleven dreams after Sarah's death, Constance reports the gradual lessening of her pain through changing dream images.

"In my fourth dream, eight months after Sarah's death, I could see myself crying over Sarah. I woke up feeling anxious and heavy at heart. A few weeks later, in my fifth dream, I knew Sarah was going to die. We were face-to-face, in deep eye contact, not blinking at all, wordlessly sharing our love for each other. I have never felt this way before. I felt content and peaceful, with a deep sense of love all through me." Constance's dreams show the slow progression of healing and the way in which her dreams help her gradually absorb the shock of her tremendous loss.

Grief Dreams Repair and Restore by Sorting Through Emotions

To be repaired and restored, our second definition of healing, is accomplished when grief dreams help us sort through our emotions. With the help of grief dreams, we feel the return of our feelings after the initial, often immobilizing, shock of grief: we are emotionally repaired and restored.

Eve writes of her deep sadness after the loss of her beloved friend Amelia. Like Constance, Eve reports a series of meaningful grief dreams—dreams she views as gifts. "Amelia comes to see me, radiant, dazzling. I am overjoyed to see her and tell her so." Eve explains that she had been depressed in the months following Amelia's death. "But," she says, "dreams of Amelia helped move my energy." Eve's dreams helped her to work through her grief and to repair her depressed feelings by restoring feelings of radiant, dazzling joy with Amelia.

Grief Dreams Settle and Restore Harmony with an Inner Relationship

To settle and restore harmony, a third definition of healing, is a welcome aspect of the denouement phase of grief. Mourners know this feeling—often described as *comfort* or *peace*—as the point when an inner sense of relationship with the deceased is restored.

Jessica describes her unsettled, uneasy feelings of grief after her brother, Adam, was tragically murdered. Her dream, one year after his death, relates a developing sense of her brother's presence within, guided by her loving husband who acts as Jessica's grief partner.

"In the dream, I am walking with my husband. He tells me to concentrate in order to feel Adam's presence (I did)." She explains that over time, the dream has helped to settle her grief and has brought comfort. The traumatic circumstances of Adam's death require Jessica's patient, long-term perspective for deep restoration and healing.

In Chapter Four, Julie's dream of her deceased brother, Bill, conducting a symphony orchestra, conveys how harmony is restored to a family torn by grief. The image of the family coming together again as Bill conducts orchestral harmony is a vivid portrayal of Julie's well-established, inner relationship with Bill.

Lisann lost her father to a heart attack before he could visit her in the home that she and her husband had built. Her dream was of meeting her father in front of her new home. Lisann's dream eases her feelings of regret that her father died before seeing her house, but on a deeper level, the dream helps Lisann forge a new connection with her father: "I believe this dream was telling me that my dad is closer than I think and that he sees our house."

Grief Dreams Bring Wholeness by Creating Bridges to the Future

To cause a person to become healthy and whole, our fourth definition of healing, fits with our description of the fourth dimension of grief dreams as life-affirming bridges to the future for survivors. Marlene describes a difficult period of grieving after the death of her beloved younger brother, Raymond, from an accidental overdose.

"Raymond was a pretty rugged guy, well-known for giving awe-some bear hugs," says Marlene. "I had a dream about Raymond about three and a half years after his death. When I saw him, I said, 'Raymond, it's really you!' We both stood up and started hugging. I remember him hugging me hard with a low growl, which he always did during a hug as a teasing, humorous thing." Marlene feels that the dream brought her a sense of wholeness: "The dream of his hug meant the world to me." And it allowed her a healing bridge into her future: "This dream really helped me to start to move on and heal."

Lisa, whom we met in Chapter Seven, lost her brother-in-law to complications following surgery. She feels confident that she will have more dreams of him: "I know he'll visit me again. I keep a picture on my desk and talk to him often, telling him how I feel." Lisa's future includes more dreams of her inner confidante—her beloved brother-in-law—that grow with her over time.

Hope

Aristotle conceived of hope as a dawning sense of trust in the future, as a *waking dream.* Another way to describe this fourth aspect of healing is a sense of hope. After the dark months of intense grief, hope emerges with a promise of future possibilities. Grief dreams often bear meaningful images of a hopeful new life for the mourner.

For example, Sarah explains that she was reassured by the symbol of a clock in her dream about her sister, Heidi, fourteen months after Heidi's suicide. Clocks in dreams represent the passage of time—the healer of all wounds, as the saying goes. Sarah writes, "I have had other dreams about my sister, but none has given me the same feeling of reassurance as this one. I'm learning to let go little by little every day." When we're grieving, the movement forward is often imperceptible, but the images in our dreams remind us that restoration is indeed taking place. Like Sarah, Lisa recounts another dream of her brother-in-law that featured the image of a calendar: "I took that as a sign to keep going." The gradual return of hope does not signal an end to mourning—for grief is the work of a lifetime—but our dreams can help us recognize that we are moving forward and that we are indeed beginning to heal.

But what if our hopes and dreams are not enough to sustain us through our grief? Healing may, at times, require professional health care.

SEEKING PROFESSIONAL HELP

We have stressed throughout the book that at some point in your grieving process, you may require the help of a medical doctor or psychotherapist. We understand grief as a normal, healthy response to the death of a loved one, but sometimes we "get stuck" and need professional help. Grief experts often call this *complicated bereavement*, which has become a term that encompasses a variety of issues. The following section is a useful guide for helping you to find appropriate health care.

Start with Your Primary Care Physician

It is always important to have a checkup with your family doctor or nurse practitioner during your initial months of grief. Your doctor or nurse can advise you on ways to take care of yourself and instruct you to watch for indications of potential health problems. These signs include physical ailments; sleep loss; depressed, irritable, or unstable mood; suicidal thoughts; flashbacks of an earlier trauma; excessive alcohol or drug use; and feeling isolated in your grief or fearing that you are burdening others. Grief experts note an increase in physical ailments during bereavement, so your medical practitioner will first rule out any physical problems that might be contributing to your difficulty. Then he or she will determine if you are suffering from complicated bereavement and will refer you for further treatment.

This may include a recommendation that you see a psychiatrist for further evaluation of your symptoms and to determine if medication or counseling with a trained professional for grief work is needed. These are two separate recommendations—a referral to a psychiatrist and a referral to a counselor—that may be confusing at first. We will clarify the distinction between these two treatments as well as other treatments to guide you through the maze of health care choices.

Psychiatric Treatment

A psychiatrist is a medical doctor trained to evaluate and treat mental health problems. A psychiatrist also prescribes medication. During grief, the most common problems brought to a psychiatrist are feelings of depression and anxiety and substance abuse. When you meet with a psychiatrist, the first session will be a discussion to evaluate your problem and decide on a treatment plan. The treatment may be medication and follow-up sessions with the psychiatrist, or the psychiatrist may suggest counseling with a therapist to talk about your difficulties.

Counseling

Counseling is an umbrella term for different ways of talking about your grief with a trained professional. There are several different kinds of counseling (also called psychotherapy) that are offered by counselors with various credentials (such as psychologist, psychiatrist, social worker, psychiatric nurse, pastoral counselor, or grief counselor), and we believe that most mourners can benefit from some type of grief counseling.

Depending on your situation, your primary care physician or nurse can often recommend a specific counselor. Or you may find one through a friend, employee benefit program, or your own research. You are likely to feel a great deal of comfort when you can express your feelings to a professional who understands what it is like to grieve. Your counselor will also provide reassurance and guidance for the days and months ahead. You can choose whether you prefer individual or family counseling or a grief group, or perhaps some combination of these. Often your health insurance will pay for this important support. Inquire if your employer offers an employee assistance program for grief counseling. (See the Reader Resources section for other helpful information.)

Mind-Body Healing

There are other treatments that focus on the relationship between psychological and physical well-being that are helpful for grief work. These therapies include massage, acupuncture, yoga, reiki, homeopathy, and holistic counseling. The Reader Resources section includes specific Web site references for further information and referral.

HOW GRIEF DREAMS HELP HEAL US: ENDNOTES

As we have maintained throughout this book, dreamers are in the best position to interpret their own dreams. It is our hope that these pages have not only provided a useful guide for empowering you to gain insight, understanding, and comfort from your grief dreams but have also helped you to realize that you are not alone. Although the journey of grief is often described as a solitary one, the dream stories in this book bear loving testimony to the fact that all of us, at one time or another, will travel that well-worn path of sorrow. We thought it fitting, therefore, to conclude this book in the style of the Greek chorus, with the collective voices of dreamers who have found hopeful consolation in their grief dreams:

- *When I think of my dream, I feel happier and hopeful about my own life.*—Julie

- *When I wake up, the dream stays with me for days. I feel happy knowing that I saw my grandmother and got to talk to her.*—Ellen

- *I think the most important part of my dream was seeing my brother. I really needed to see him, and he showed me that he was OK. He gave me a little humorous turn from side to side so I could get a good look.*—Cory

- *I had been worried that I would forget what my brother looked like or the sound of his voice—but it was all so clear in front of me, and it was his voice, I hadn't forgotten at all! This was one of the most moving dreams I had; it made me wake up feeling so happy.*—Rachel

- *This dream is my subconscious trying to find peace for my grief.*—Jessica

- *His dream visits have helped me to work through my grief. I know that he is here in spirit and I know that I'll be with him again someday. These dreams have truly been a blessing because they have given me the chance to spend time with my brother, to hug him, and tell him I love him—and I get it all back from him—all the things we didn't really express when he was alive.*—Tara

- *The dream I had has been helpful in allowing me to move on in my grief process of letting go of guilt and responsibility for my sister's suicide.*—Sue

- *I felt it was a blessing to be able to dream of my daughter. That at least in my dreams I can see her. And I thanked the Lord.*—Constance

- *I continue to miss Amelia terribly and always look forward to hearing from her.*—Eve

- *One thing I know for sure is that he's not in pain anymore and he's still with us. Each day brings different feelings as it does with everyone. I haven't had any more dreams, but I know he'll visit me again.*—Lisa

- *I woke up remembering the sound of her laughter. I felt elated, as if I had received one more visit, and the joy of this dream stayed with me for days.*—Joyce

Oprah Winfrey has reflected that every one of us is the keeper of a dream. The dreamkeepers of this book elaborate on Oprah's wisdom using a full palette of dreamscapes: visitation, message, reassurance, trauma, combination, intentional, lucid, series, prophetic, and all the other dreams paint a vibrant witness to the healing power of grief dreams.

Reader Resources

The following are some resources that may be helpful to the reader. For each chapter, there are both recommended readings and Web resources. (Specific Web addresses appear within brackets.)

Chapter One: The Journey of Grief—Recommended Reading

Attig, Thomas. *How We Grieve: Relearning the World.* New York: Oxford University Press, 1996. (Attig's work on meaning making is both sensitive and immensely practical.)

Bonsib, Sandy. *Quilting Your Memories: Inspirations for Designing with Image Transfers.* Woodinville, Wash.: Martingale, 1999. (This is an excellent book to help you create a memory scrapbook honoring your loved one.)

Christensen, Alice. *The American Yoga Association Beginner's Manual.* New York: Fireside, 2002. (This particular book is accessible and helpful even to the novice.)

Coughlin, Ruth. *Grieving: A Love Story.* New York: Random House, 1993.

Doka, Kenneth J. *Disenfranchised Grief: New Directions, Challenges, and Strategies for Practice.* Ontario: Research Press, 2002.

Frankl, Viktor E. *Man's Search for Meaning.* New York: Washington Square Press, 1998.

Grollman, Earl. *What Helped Me When My Loved One Died.* Boston: Beacon Press, 1981. (Grollman is a widely read bereavement author and has published several excellent grief books.)

James, John W., and Russell Friedman. *The Grief Recovery Handbook.* New York: HarperCollins, 1998.

Kübler-Ross, Elisabeth. *On Death and Dying*. Old Tappan, N.J.: Macmillan, 1969. (Kübler-Ross's pioneering work on death, dying, and grief is detailed in this, her first, book.)

Lewis, C. S. *A Grief Observed*. New York: Bantam Books, 1983. (This book is based on Lewis's experience after losing his wife.)

Rando, Therese A. *How to Go on Living When Someone You Love Dies*. New York: Bantam Books, 1988. (Rando discusses a variety of losses in an easy-to-read, compassionate style.)

Remen, Rachel Naomi. *Kitchen Table Wisdom*. New York: Riverhead Books. 1996.

Roche, Lorin. *Meditation Made Easy*. San Francisco: HarperSanFrancisco, 1998. (This book is helpful for those looking for relief from some of the more distressing symptoms of grief, such as anger, fear, and worry.)

Sanders, Catherine M. *Surviving Grief . . . and Learning to Live Again*. New York: Wiley, 1992.

Slan, Joanna Campbell. *Scrapbook Storytelling: Save Family Stories and Memories with Photos, Journaling, and Your Own Creativity*. St. Louis: EFG, 1999. (This is a great guide for beginners and experts alike.)

Smedley, Wendy. *The Complete Idiot's Guide to Scrapbooks*. Indianapolis: Alpha Books, 2000.

Solomon, Andrew. *The Noonday Demon: An Atlas of Depression*. New York: Scribner, 2001. (Solomon's book is a popular resource for those who wish to learn more about depression.)

Wolfelt, Alan D. *Death and Grief: A Guide for Clergy*. Muncie, Ind.: Accelerated Development, 1988. (Although the name implies that this book is for clergy, Wolfelt's books are very readable and helpful for anyone who has suffered a loss. His discussion of grief-related depression versus major depression is informative and helpful.)

Wray, T. J. *Surviving the Death of a Sibling: Living Through Grief When an Adult Brother or Sister Dies*. New York: Three Rivers Press, 2003. (Although this book is primarily for surviving adult siblings, it's full of practical self-help steps for any mourner.)

Wright, Jesse H., and Monica Ramirez Basco. *Getting Your Life Back: The Complete Guide to Recovery from Depression*. New York: Free Press, 2001. (This is a solid, comprehensive guide.)

Zieman, Nancy. *10–20–30 Minutes to Quilt*. Birmingham, Ala.: Oxmoor House, 2000. (This is an excellent resource for those interested in creating a memory quilt to honor their loved one.)

Chapter One: The Journey of Grief—Web Resources

Institute for the Study and Treatment of Loss: [www.thereserando.com]. (This
    site provides mental health services through psychotherapy, training,
    supervision, and consultation. It specializes in loss and grief, traumatic
    stress, and the psychosocial care of persons with chronic, life-threatening,
    or terminal illness and their loved ones.)

National Funeral Directors Association: [www.nfda.org/mediacenter/nfdafact.
    html]. (See this site for help in planning a funeral.)

Willowgreen: [www.willowgreen.com/cust_AdviceDisplay.asp?TextTypeID
    =30&List=Grief]. (This site is geared to men dealing with grief.)

The following sites offer support after the loss of a child:

Bereaved Parents of the U.S.A.: [www.bereavedparentsusa.org].

Compassionate Friends: [www.compassionatefriends.org]. (The largest grief orga-
    nization in America provides grief information and instructions for find-
    ing support. Most members are bereaved parents.)

Healing Hearts–Bereaved Parents: [www.healingheart.net].

Mothers Against Drunk Driving (MADD): [www.madd.org].

Parents of Murdered Children: [www.pomc.com].

Source of Help in Airing and Resolving Experience: [www.nationalshareoffice.
    com].

Sudden Infant Death Syndrome (SIDS) and Other Infant Death:
    [www.SIDS-network.org].

The following sites offer support for widowed persons:

National Association of Widows: [www.widows.uk.net].

Young Widows: [www.youngwidows.org].

The following sites deal with depression:

Bipolar Disorder Digest: [www.lorenbennett.org]. (This site discusses the symp-
    toms of depression.)

Counseling for Loss and Life Changes: [www.counselingforloss.com]. (At this
    site, you can talk about depression and obtain further information.)

Depression Screening: [www.depression-screening.org]. (You can screen yourself
    for depression at this site.)

National Foundation for Depressive Illness: [www.depression.org]. (Go to this
    site for information on depression and therapies, including medications.)

National Mental Health Association: [www.nmha.org].(This site discusses the symptoms of depression.)

The following sites offer help with meaning making:

Create a Video: [www.createavideo.com]. (Contact this site to create a video memorial.)

Growing Through Grief: [www.growingthroughgrief.com]. (This site is dedicated to the emotional healing of the bereaved through music and a series of audio recordings designed to help mourners rebuild their lives after a loss.)

My Heart Is Missing: [www.myheartsmissinglink.com]. (For an external symbol of mourning, you can order a heart-shaped pendant—with a "missing link" and your loved one's birthstone in the center—to wear as an external symbol of mourning and loss.)

Scrapbook Tips: [www.scrapbook-tips.com]. (Go to this site for on-line scrapbook help.)

Chapter Two: About Dreams—Recommended Reading

Bosnak, Robert. *A Little Course in Dreams*. Boston: Shambhala, 1988. (Both of Bosnak's books are helpful in developing a more comprehensive understanding of dreams and dreamwork.)

Bosnak, Robert. *Tracks in the Wilderness of Dreaming: Exploring Interior Landscape Through Practical Dreamwork*. New York: Delta Books, 1996.

Campbell, Joseph, ed. *The Portable Jung*. New York: Viking Penguin, 1971. (Campbell provides a clear overview of Jung's work.)

Campbell, Joseph, with Bill Moyers. *The Power of Myth*. New York: Doubleday, 1988. (This is an entertaining and informative book that will help illuminate the concept of archetype. It is also available on video and DVD.)

Ellenberger, Henri F. *The Discovery of the Unconscious*. New York: Basic Books, 1970.

Freud, Sigmund. *The Interpretation of Dreams*. In *The Basic Writings of Sigmund Freud*. Translated and edited, with an Introduction by A. A. Brill. New York: Random House, 1966.

Godwin, Gail. *Heart*. New York: HarperCollins, 2001. (Godwin provides a book-length amplification of the symbolic meaning of *heart*.)

Hopcke, Robert H. *A Guided Tour of the Collected Works of C. G. Jung*. Boston: Shambhala, 1989.

Jung, C. G. *The Collected Works of C. G. Jung*. 20 vols. Princeton, N.J.: Princeton University Press, 1956–1969.

Jung, C. G. *Memories, Dreams, Reflections*. New York: Vintage Books, 1989.

Mitchell, Stephen A., and Margaret J. Black. *Freud and Beyond: A History of Modern Psychoanalytic Thought*. New York: Basic Books, 1995.

Samuels, Andrew. *Jung and the Post-Jungians*. New York: Routledge, 1994.

Singer, June. *Boundaries of the Soul: The Practice of Jung's Psychology*. New York: Doubleday, 1994.

Stevens, Anthony. *Private Myths: Dreams and Dreaming*. Cambridge, Mass.: Harvard University Press, 1995.

Whitmont, Edward C., and Sylvia Brinton Perera. *Dreams: A Portal to the Source*. New York: Routledge, 1989.

Chapter Two: About Dreams—Web Resources

Association for the Study of Dreams: [www.asdreams.org]. (This is an international, multidisciplinary organization dedicated to the pure and applied investigation of dreams and dreaming.)

C. G. Jung Institute of Boston: [www.cgjungboston.com]. (This Web site offers information about the practice and training of Jungian analysis in the northeastern United States. It also provides links to all Jung Institutes. This site is a good starting point if you wish to consult a Jungian analyst or to pursue opportunities for studying Jungian psychology.)

Dream Emporium: [www.dreamemporium.com]. (This site features basic dream information, including types of dreams and tips for keeping a dream journal.)

Grief Dreams: [www.griefdreams.com]. (This unique grief dream site, created by author T. J. Wray, features information, message board, and chat.)

International Association of Analytical Psychology: [www.iaap.org]. (The International Association for Analytical Psychology was founded in 1955 and is the accrediting and regulatory organization for all professional analytical psychologists' groups. This site offers information about the theory and practice of Jungian psychology as well as an international list of contact information for all member Jungian psychoanalysts.)

International Institute for Dream Research: [www.dreamresearch.ca/]. (This site features information and a "dream bank," where dreamers can submit their dreams for analysis.)

Temple of Dreams: [www.templeofdreams.com/teaching.html]. (This is an excellent site for historical information about dreams.)

Chapter Three: The Visitation Dream—
Recommended Reading

Bosnak, Robert. *A Little Course in Dreams*. Boston: Shambhala, 1988.

Delaney, Gayle. *New Directions in Dream Interpretation*. Albany: State University of New York Press, 1993.

The following sources offer information on dream dictionaries. Although there are many excellent dream dictionaries available both on-line and in print, we find the following most helpful:

Cirlot, J. E. *A Dictionary of Symbols*. 2nd ed. New York: Philosophical Library, 1971. (This is a scholarly dream dictionary that uses the comparative method, specifying sources from a wide variety of fields.)

Crisp, Tony. *Dream Dictionary: An A to Z Guide to Understanding Your Unconscious Mind*. New York: Dell, 2002. (This is a well-researched, user-friendly paperback dream dictionary with helpful theoretical explanations and an excellent bibliography.)

DeVries, Ad. *Dictionary of Symbols and Imagery*. New York: Elsevier, 1984. (This is the definitive, unabridged symbol dictionary.)

Holloway, Gillian. *The Complete Dream Book: Discover What Your Dreams Tell About You and Your Life*. Napierville, Ill.: Sourcebooks, 2001. (Holloway has written a well-documented guidebook, organized by dream topic, that explains how to understand your dreams for your everyday life.)

Matthews, Boris, trans. *The Herder Dictionary of Symbols*. Wilmette, Ill.: Chiron, 1993. (Originally published in 1978 as *Herder Lexikon: Symbole*, by Herder Freiburg.) (This is a pocket-sized, quick, authoritative reference.)

Parker, Derek, and Julia Parker. *The Complete Book of Dreams*. New York: Dorling Kindersley, 1995. (The Parkers have put together an illustrated dream reference book that is organized by dream themes. The index is a dream thesaurus that lists basic dream images with suggested related themes.)

Robinson, Lady Stearn, and Tom Corbett. *The Dreamer's Dictionary*. New York: Warner Books, 1974. (This dream dictionary is very user-friendly and easy to read and understand.)

Schoenewolf, Gerald. *A Dictionary of Dream Interpretation*. Northvale, N.J.: Aronson, 1997. (Although this work is a bit scholarly, it is still very good.)

Zucker, Fiona. *Dream Decoder: Reveal Your Unconscious Desires*. New York: Quarto, 2000. (This is a beautifully illustrated book that uses colors as a framework for understanding dream symbols.)

Chapter Three: The Visitation Dream—Web Resources

American Association of Suicidology: [www.suicidology.org/].

Dream Moods: [www.dreammoods.com/]. (Among other things, this site features an on-line dream dictionary and tips to help you better recall your dreams.)

Grief Dreams: [www.griefdreams.com]. (This unique grief dream site, created by author T. J. Wray, features information, message board, and chat.)

Chapter Four: The Message Dream—Recommended Reading

Cirlot, J. E. *A Dictionary of Symbols*. 2nd ed. New York: Philosophical Library, 1971.

Crisp, Tony. *Dream Dictionary: An A to Z Guide to Understanding Your Unconscious Mind*. New York: Dell, 2002.

DeVries, Ad. *Dictionary of Symbols and Imagery*. New York: Elsevier, 1984.

Hamilton-Parker, Craig. *Remembering and Understanding Your Dreams*. New York: Sterling, 2000.

Leonard, Linda Schierse. *Creation's Heartbeat*. New York: Bantam Books, 1995. (Based on her own message dream of healing and hope, this Jungian analyst helps the reader realize the power of message dreams.)

Mattoon, Mary Ann. *Understanding Dreams*. Woodstock, Conn.: Spring, 1984.

Souza, Susan Mello, with Joanne Harrington. *The Same Smile: The Triumph of a Mother's Love After Losing Two Daughters*. Baltimore: Gateway Press, 2002. (This lovely book will enable you to learn more about Susan and her daughter Jackie.)

Zucker, Fiona. *Dream Decoder: Reveal Your Unconscious Desires*. New York: Quarto, 2000.

Chapter Four: The Message Dream—Web Resources

Counseling for Loss and Life Changes: [www.counselingforloss.com/article5.html] and [www.counselingforloss.com/article11.html]. (These articles are helpful for coping with grief during the holidays.)

Grief Dreams: [www.griefdreams.com]. (This unique grief dream site, created by author T. J. Wray, features information, message board, and chat.)

Same Smile: [www.thesamesmile.com]. (At this site, you can learn more about Susan and Jackie.)

Chapter Five: The Reassurance Dream—Recommended Reading

Bolen, Jean Shinoda. *Goddesses in Everywoman*. New York: HarperCollins, 1984.

Bolen, Jean Shinoda. *Gods in Everyman*. New York: HarperCollins, 1989.

Cirlot, J. E. *A Dictionary of Symbols*. 2nd ed. New York: Philosophical Library, 1971.

Crisp, Tony. *Dream Dictionary: An A to Z Guide to Understanding Your Unconscious Mind*. New York: Dell, 2002.

DeVries, Ad. *Dictionary of Symbols and Imagery*. New York: Elsevier, 1984.

Hamilton-Parker, Craig. *Remembering and Understanding Your Dreams*. New York: Sterling, 2000.

Mattoon, Mary Ann. *Understanding Dreams*. Woodstock, Conn.: Spring, 1984.

Robinson, Lady Stearn, and Tom Corbett. *The Dreamer's Dictionary*. New York: Warner Books, 1974.

Schoenewolf, Gerald. *A Dictionary of Dream Interpretation*. Northvale, N.J.: Aronson, 1997.

Chapter Five: The Reassurance Dream—Web Resources

Grief Dreams: [www.griefdreams.com]. (This unique grief dream site, created by author T. J. Wray, features information, message board, and chat.)

Grief, Loss, and Recovery: [www.grieflossrecovery.com/]. (The site offers emotional support and friendship and provides a safe place for the bereaved to share feelings.)

GriefNet-Rivendell Resources: [www.rivendell.org/]. (Here you can find a variety of resources related to death, dying, bereavement, and major emotional and physical losses.)

Chapter Six: The Trauma Dream—Recommended Reading

Barrett, Deirdre, ed. *Trauma and Dreams*. Cambridge, Mass.: Harvard University Press, 1996. (This is an essential contribution to dream research.)

Bly, Robert, and Marion Woodman. *The Maiden King*. New York: Henry Holt, 1998.

Bosnak, Robert. *Dreaming with an AIDS Patient*. Boston: Shambhala, 1989.

Bulkeley, Kelly. *Dreams of Healing: Transforming Nightmares into Visions of Hope*. Mahwah, N.J.: Paulist Press, 2003. (Based on post–9-11 nightmares, this book takes a sensitive, healing approach to nightmares. It is well written and highly readable.)

Cirlot, J. E. *A Dictionary of Symbols*. 2nd ed. New York: Philosophical Library, 1971.

Crisp, Tony. *Dream Dictionary: An A to Z Guide to Understanding Your Unconscious Mind*. New York: Dell, 2002.

DeVries, Ad. *Dictionary of Symbols and Imagery*. New York: Elsevier, 1984.

Hamilton-Parker, Craig. *Remembering and Understanding Your Dreams*. New York: Sterling, 2000.

Kalsched, Donald. *The Inner World of Trauma: Archetypal Defenses of the Personal Spirit*. New York: Routledge, 1996.

Sanford, John. *Dreams and Healing*. Mahwah, N.J.: Paulist Press, 1979.

Wheelwright, Jane Hollister. *The Death of a Woman: How a Life Became Complete*. New York: St. Martin's Press, 1981.

Chapter Six: The Trauma Dream—Web Resources

AirCraft Casualty Emotional Support Services: [www.accesshelp.org/]. (This site provides peer grief support and information to those who have lost loved ones in air disasters.)

American Association of Suicidology: [www.suicidology.org/].

Doors of Hope: [www.doorsofhope.com/]. (This site provides support, healing, and help for victims of abuse, bullying, violence, and the sudden death of a loved one.)

Grief Dreams: [www.griefdreams.com]. (This unique grief dream site, created by author T. J. Wray, features information, message board, and chat.)

HALOS: [www.halos.org]. (This is a support resource for family and friends who have lost a loved one to homicide.)

Institute for the Study and Treatment of Loss: [www.thereserando.com]. (This site provides mental health services through psychotherapy, training, supervision, and consultation. It specializes in loss and grief, traumatic stress, and the psychosocial care of persons with chronic, life-threatening, or terminal illness and their loved ones.)

National Center for Post-Traumatic Stress Disorder: [www.ncptsd.org/].

National Organization for Victim Assistance: [www.try-nova.org/]. (There is also a twenty-four-hour hot line: 202-393-6683.)

Tragedy Assistance Program for Survivors: [www.taps.org]. (This is a resource for
those who have lost a loved one who was serving in the armed forces.)

Wendt Center for Loss and Healing: [www.lossandhealing.org]. (This is a site for
the support of survivors of the sudden and traumatic death of a loved one.)

Chapter Seven: Other Types of Grief Dreams—Recommended Reading

Bletzer, June G. *Encyclopedic Psychic Dictionary*. 3rd ed. Lithia Springs, Ga.:
New Leaf, 1998.

Bosnak, Robert. *Tracks in the Wilderness of Dreaming: Exploring Interior Landscape
Through Practical Dreamwork*. New York: Delta Books, 1996.

Browne, Sylvia. *Sylvia Browne's Book of Dreams*. New York: Signet Books, 2003.

Cirlot, J. E. *A Dictionary of Symbols*. 2nd ed. New York: Philosophical Library, 1971.

Crisp, Tony. *Dream Dictionary: An A to Z Guide to Understanding Your Unconscious Mind*. New York: Dell, 2002.

DeVries, Ad. *Dictionary of Symbols and Imagery*. New York: Elsevier, 1984.

Edward, John. *One Last Time: A Medium Speaks to Those Who Have Loved and
Lost*. New York: Berkley, 2000.

Edward, John. *After Life: Answers from the Other Side*. New York: Princess Books,
2003.

Gad, Irene. *Tarot and Individuation: Correspondences with Cabala and Alchemy*.
York Beach, Maine: Nicolas-Hays, 1994.

Godwin, Gail. *Heart*. New York: HarperCollins, 2001.

Robinson, Lady Stearn, and Tom Corbett. *The Dreamer's Dictionary*. New York:
Warner Books, 1974.

Roob, Alexander. *Alchemy and Mysticism: The Hermetic Museum*. New York:
Taschen, 1997.

Shepard, Leslie A., ed. *Encyclopedia of Occultism and Parapsychology*. Detroit:
Gale Research, 1991.

Ullman, Montague, Stanley Krippner, and Alan Vaughn. *Dream Telepathy:
Experiments in Nocturnal Extrasensory Perception*. 2nd ed. Jefferson, N.C.:
McFarland, 1989.

Van Praagh, James. *Healing Grief: Reclaiming Life After Loss*. New York:
NAL/Dutton, 2000.

Chapter Seven: Other Types of Grief Dreams—Web Resources

Myths-Dreams-Symbols: [mythsdreamssymbols.com/precognitivedreams.html].
(See this site for an excellent on-line article about prophetic dreaming.)

Prophetic Dreams and Visions (for America): [www.pressie.org/dreams_visions. html]. (This site features the prophetic dream stories of both famous Americans and average citizens.)

Chapter Eight: Faith and Grief Dreams— Recommended Reading

Aycock, Don. M. *Prayer 101: What It Is, What It Isn't, How to Do It*. Nashville, Tenn.: Broadman and Holman, 1998.

Benson, Herbert. *Timeless Healing: The Power and Biology of Belief*. New York: Scribner, 1996.

Blumenthal, David R. *Facing the Abusing God*. Louisville, Ky.: Westminster John Knox, 1993.

Crisp, Tony. *Dream Dictionary: An A to Z Guide to Understanding Your Unconscious Mind*. New York: Dell, 2002.

Kushner, Harold S. *When Bad Things Happen to Good People*. New York: Avon, 1981. (In this classic book in bereavement studies, Kushner takes on the question of theodicy following the death of his son. This book has helped millions to cope with the loss of a loved one.)

Lewis, C. S. *A Grief Observed*. New York: Bantam Books, 1983.

Mosley, Glenn, and Joanna Hill. *The Power of Prayer Around the World*. Radnor, Penn.: Templeton Foundation Press, 2000.

O'Connor, Peter. *Dreams and the Search for Meaning*. Mahwah, N.J.: Paulist Press, 1987.

O'Malley, William. *God: The Oldest Question*. Chicago: Loyola Press, 2000. (This lively, well-written, and engaging book is excellent for those who have struggled with their faith.)

Postema, Don. *Space for God: The Study and Practice of Prayer and Spirituality*. Grand Rapids, Mich.: CRC Publications, 1997.

Sanford, John A. *Dreams and Healing*. Mahwah, N.J.: Paulist Press, 1979.

Sanford, John A. *Dreams: God's Forgotten Language*. San Francisco: HarperSanFrancisco, 1989.

Sharpe, Jonathan. *Divining Your Dreams: How the Ancient Mystical Tradition of the Kabbalah Can Help You Interpret More Than 850 Powerful Dream Images*. New York: Simon & Schuster, 2002.

Steinpach, Richard. *Why We Live After Death*. Gambier, Ohio: Grail Foundation Press, 1979.

Chapter Eight: Faith and Grief Dreams—Web Resources

HoyWeb.Com: [www.hoyweb.com/faq/griefrec.htm]. (See this site for information about grief and faith from a Christian perspective.)

IslamOnline.net: [www.islamonline.net/English/introducingislam/Worship/Heart/article05.shtml]. (See this site for information about grief and faith from a Muslim perspective.)

Mishpacha: [www.mishpacha.org/deathintro.shtml]. (See this site for information about grief and faith from a Jewish perspective.)

Myths-Dreams-Symbols: [www.mythsdreamssymbols.com/jung spirituality.html]. (See this site for an on-line article about dreams and spirituality.)

Chapter Nine: How Grief Dreams Help Heal Us— Recommended Reading

Bosnak, Robert. *A Little Course in Dreams*. Boston: Shambhala, 1988.

Bosnak, Robert. *Tracks in the Wilderness of Dreaming: Exploring Interior Landscape Through Practical Dreamwork*. New York: Delta Books, 1996.

Cirlot, J. E. *A Dictionary of Symbols*. 2nd ed. New York: Philosophical Library, 1971.

Cousins, Norman. *Anatomy of an Illness as Perceived by the Patient*. New York: Norton, 1979.

Crisp, Tony. *Dream Dictionary: An A to Z Guide to Understanding Your Unconscious Mind*. New York: Dell, 2002.

DeVries, Ad. *Dictionary of Symbols and Imagery*. New York: Elsevier, 1984.

Estes, Clarissa Pinkola. *Women Who Run with the Wolves*. New York: Ballantine, 1992.

Ganin, Barbara. *Art and Healing: Using Expressive Art to Heal Your Body, Mind, and Spirit*. New York: Three Rivers Press, 1999.

Hillman, James, and Margot McLean. *Dream Animals*. San Francisco: Chronicle Books, 1997.

Jung, C. G. *The Collected Works of C. G. Jung*. 20 vols. Princeton, N.J.: Princeton University Press, 1956–1969.

Jung, C. G. *Memories, Dreams, Reflections*. New York: Random House, 1961.

Kabat-Zinn, Jon. *Full Catastrophe Living*. New York: Bantam Books, 1990.

Leonard, Linda Schierse. *Creation's Heartbeat*. New York: Bantam Books, 1995.

Moyers, Bill. *Healing and the Mind*. New York: Doubleday, 1993.

Remen, Rachel Naomi. *Kitchen Table Wisdom*. New York: Riverhead Books, 1996.

Solomon, Andrew. *The Noonday Demon: An Atlas of Depression.* New York: Scribner, 2001.

Wolfelt, Alan D. *Death and Grief: A Guide for Clergy.* Muncie, Ind.: Accelerated Development, 1988.

Chapter Nine: How Grief Dreams Help Heal Us— Web Resources

Adult Sibling Grief: [www.adultsiblinggrief.com]. (This Web site, created by author T. J. Wray, is dedicated to surviving adult siblings. It provides a message board, chat, and memorials.)

American Holistic Health Association: [www.ahha.org]. (Contact this organization for holistic health information.)

American Integrative Medicine Association/Association for Integrative Health Care Practitioners: [www.aihcp-norfolkva.org/]. (This site can help you find credentialed and certified integrative health care practitioners specializing in complementary and alternative medicine or health care.)

American Psychiatric Association: [www.psych.org].

American Psychological Association: [www.apa.org].

Association for Death Education and Counseling: [www.adec.org]. (See this site for help in choosing a therapist.)

Compassionate Friends: [www.compassionatefriends.org]. (The largest grief organization in America provides grief information and instructions for finding support. Most members are bereaved parents.)

Crisis, Grief, and Healing: [www.webhealing.com/]. (This site specializes in healing from loss.)

Doors of Hope: [www.doorsofhope.com/]. (This site provides support, healing, and help for victims of abuse, bullying, violence, and the sudden death of a loved one.)

Grief, Loss, and Recovery: [www.grieflossrecovery.com/]. (The site offers emotional support and friendship and provides a safe place for the bereaved to share feelings.)

GriefNet-Rivendell Resources: [www.rivendell.org/]. (Here you can find a variety of resources related to death, dying, bereavement, and major emotional and physical losses.)

Growth House: [www.growthhouse.org]. (This site is for the bereaved and those who care for them.)

GROWW: [www.groww.com/]. (GROWW offers a wide range of grief and bereavement resources.)

Hospice Foundation of America: [www.hospicefoundation.org/]. (The site provides death, dying, and bereavement services.)

Institute for the Study and Treatment of Loss: [www.thereserando .com]. (This
site provides mental health services through psychotherapy, training,
supervision, and consultation. It specializes in loss and grief, traumatic
stress, and the psychosocial care of persons with chronic, life-threatening,
or terminal illness and their loved ones.)

OfSpirit.com: [www.ofspirit.com]. (This site offers information on mind-body
healing.)

Psych Central: [www.psychcentral.com/therapst.html]. (See this site for help in
choosing a therapist.)

Selected Sources

Chapter One

Attig, Thomas. *How We Grieve: Relearning the World*. New York: Oxford University Press, 1996.

Bonsib, Sandy. *Quilting Your Memories: Inspirations for Designing with Image Transfers*. Woodinville, Wash.: Martingale, 1999.

Bowlby, John J. *Separation: Anxiety and Anger*. Vol. 2. *Attachment and Loss*. London: Hogarth Press, 1973.

Bowlby, John J. *Loss: Sadness and Depression*. Vol. 3. *Attachment and Loss*. London: Hogarth Press, 1980.

Bowlby, John J. *Attachment*. Vol. 1, 2nd ed. *Attachment and Loss*. London: Hogarth Press, 1982.

Christensen, Alice. *The American Yoga Association Beginner's Manual*. New York: Fireside, 2002.

Doka, Kenneth J. *Disenfranchised Grief: New Directions, Challenges, and Strategies for Practice*. Ontario: Research Press, 2002.

Finkbeiner, Ann K. *After the Death of a Child: Living with Loss Through the Years*. New York: Free Press, 1996.

Frankl, Viktor E. *Man's Search for Meaning*. New York: Washington Square Press, 1998.

Fry, Virginia Lynn. *Part of Me Died, Too. Stories of Creative Survival Among Bereaved Children and Teenagers*. New York: Dutton Children's Books, 1995.

Grollman, Earl. *What Helped Me When My Loved One Died*. Boston: Beacon Press, 1981.

Grollman, Earl. *A Time Remembered: A Journal for Survivors*. Boston: Beacon Press, 1987.

James, John W., and Russell Friedman. *The Grief Recovery Handbook*. New York: HarperCollins, 1998.

Kübler-Ross, Elisabeth. *On Death and Dying*. Old Tappan, N.J.: Macmillan, 1969.

Lewis, C. S. *A Grief Observed*. New York: Bantam Books, 1983.

Neimeyer, Robert A., ed. *Meaning Reconstruction and the Experience of Loss*. Washington, D.C.: American Psychological Association, 2001.

Rando, Therese A. *How to Go on Living When Someone You Love Dies*. New York: Bantam Books, 1988.

Roche, Lorin. *Meditation Made Easy*. San Francisco: HarperSanFrancisco, 1998.

Rosof, Barbara D. *The Worst Loss. How Families Heal from the Death of a Child*. New York: Henry Holt, 1994.

Slan, Joanna Campbell. *Scrapbook Storytelling: Save Family Stories and Memories with Photos, Journaling, and Your Own Creativity*. St. Louis: EFG, 1999.

Smedley, Wendy. *The Complete Idiot's Guide to Scrapbooks*. Indianapolis: Alpha Books, 2000.

Solomon, Andrew. *The Noonday Demon: An Atlas of Depression*. New York: Scribner, 2001.

Wolfelt, Alan D. *Death and Grief: A Guide for Clergy*. Muncie, Ind.: Accelerated Development, 1988.

Wray, T. J. *Surviving the Death of a Sibling: Living Through Grief When an Adult Brother or Sister Dies*. New York: Three Rivers Press, 2003.

Wright, Jesse H., and Monica Ramirez Basco. *Getting Your Life Back: The Complete Guide to Recovery from Depression*. New York: Free Press, 2001.

Young-Eisendrath, Polly. *The Gifts of Suffering*. Reading, Mass.: Addison-Wesley, 1996.

Chapter Two

Barrett, Deirdre, ed. *Trauma and Dreams*. Cambridge, Mass.: Harvard University Press, 1996.

Bosnak, Robert. *Tracks in the Wilderness of Dreaming: Exploring Interior Landscape Through Practical Dreamwork*. New York: Delta Books, 1996.

Bulkeley, Kelly. *Dreams of Healing: Transforming Nightmares into Visions of Hope*. Mahwah, N.J.: Paulist Press, 2003.

Campbell, Joseph. *The Hero with a Thousand Faces*. Princeton, N.J.: Princeton University Press, 1972.

Campbell, Joseph, with Bill Moyers. *The Power of Myth*. New York: Doubleday, 1988.

Domhoff, G. William. "Making Sense of Dreaming." *Science* 299 (March 28, 2003).

Edinger, Edward. *Ego and Archetype*. Boston: Shambhala Publications, 1992.

Ellenberger, Henri F. *The Discovery of the Unconscious*. New York: Basic Books. 1970.

Foulkes, D. *Children's Dreams*. New York, Wiley, 1982.

Freud, Sigmund. *The Interpretation of Dreams*. In *The Basic Writings of Sigmund Freud*. Translated and edited, with an Introduction by A. A. Brill. New York: Random House, 1966.

Frey-Rohn, Liliane. *From Freud to Jung*. New York: Putnam, 1974.

Grant, Michael, and John Hazel. *Who's Who in Classical Mythology*. New York: Oxford University Press, 1993.

Hobson, J. Allan. *Dreaming: An Introduction to the Science of Sleep*. New York: Oxford University Press, 2002.

Jacobi, Jolande. *Complex, Archetype, Symbol*. Princeton, N.J.: Princeton University Press, 1959.

Jung, C. G. *The Collected Works of C. G. Jung*. 20 vols. Princeton, N.J.: Princeton University Press, 1956–1969.

Jung, C. G. *Dream Analysis*. Princeton, N.J.: Princeton University Press, 1984.

Jung, C. G. *Memories, Dreams, Reflections*. New York: Vintage Books, 1989.

Leeming, David Adams. *Mythology: The Voyage of the Hero*. 3rd ed. Oxford: Oxford University Press, 1998.

Maquet, Pierre, and Perrine Ruby. "Insight and the Sleep Committee." *Nature* 427 (January 22, 2004).

Mattoon, Mary Ann. *Understanding Dreams*. Woodstock, Conn.: Spring, 1984.

Parker, Derek, and Julia Parker. *The Complete Book of Dreams*. New York: Dorling Kindersley, 1995.

Propp, Vladimir. *Morphology of the Folktale*. Austin, Tex.: University of Texas Press, 1968.

Samuels, Andrew. *Jung and the Post-Jungians*. New York: Routledge, 1994.

Schectman, Jacqueline. *The Stepmother in Fairy Tales: Bereavement and the Feminine Shadow*. Boston: Sigo Press, 1993.

Siegel, Jerome M. "The REM Sleep–Memory Consolidation Hypothesis." *Science* 294 (November 2, 2001).

Stein, Murray. *Jung's Map of the Soul*. Chicago: Open Court, 1998.

Storr, Anthony. *The Essential Jung*. Princeton, N.J.: Princeton University Press, 1983.

Whitmont, Edward C. *The Symbolic Quest*. Princeton, N.J.: Princeton University Press, 1969.

Whitmont, Edward C., and Sylvia Brinton Perera. *Dreams: A Portal to the Source*. New York: Routledge, 1989.

Chapter Three

Bosnak, Robert. *A Little Course in Dreams*. Boston: Shambhala, 1988.

Bosnak, Robert. *Tracks in the Wilderness of Dreaming: Exploring Interior Landscape Through Practical Dreamwork*. New York: Delta Books, 1996.

Cirlot, J. E. *A Dictionary of Symbols*. 2nd ed. New York: Philosophical Library, 1971.

Crisp, Tony. *Dream Dictionary: An A to Z Guide to Understanding Your Unconscious Mind*. New York: Dell, 2002.

DeVries, Ad. *Dictionary of Symbols and Imagery*. New York: Elsevier, 1984.

Estes, Clarissa Pinkola. *Women Who Run with the Wolves*. New York: Ballantine, 1992.

Hillman, James. *The Dream and the Underworld*. New York: HarperCollins, 1979.

Hillman, James, and Margot McLean. *Dream Animals*. San Francisco: Chronicle Books, 1997.

Holloway, Gillian. *The Complete Dream Book: Discover What Your Dreams Tell About You and Your Life*. Napierville, Ill.: Sourcebooks, 2001.

Jung, C. G. *The Collected Works of C. G. Jung*. 20 vols. Princeton, N.J.: Princeton University Press, 1956–1969.

Mattoon, Mary Ann. *Understanding Dreams*. Woodstock, Conn.: Spring, 1984.

Schoenewolf, Gerald. *A Dictionary of Dream Interpretation*. Northvale, N.J.: Aronson, 1997.

Chapter Four

Cirlot, J. E. *A Dictionary of Symbols*. 2nd ed. New York: Philosophical Library, 1971.

Crisp, Tony. *Dream Dictionary: An A to Z Guide to Understanding Your Unconscious Mind*. New York: Dell, 2002.

DeVries, Ad. *Dictionary of Symbols and Imagery*. New York: Elsevier, 1984.

Jung, C. G. *The Collected Works of C. G. Jung*. 20 vols. Princeton, N.J.: Princeton University Press, 1956–1969.

Mattoon, Mary Ann. *Understanding Dreams*. Woodstock, Conn.: Spring, 1984.

Schoenewolf, Gerald. *A Dictionary of Dream Interpretation*. Northvale, N.J.: Aronson, 1997.

Chapter Five

Bulfinch, Thomas, with Richard P. Martin. *Bulfinch's Mythology*. New York: HarperCollins, 1991.

Cirlot, J. E. *A Dictionary of Symbols*. 2nd ed. New York: Philosophical Library, 1971.

Crim, Keith. *The Perennial Dictionary of World Religions*. San Francisco: HarperSanFrancisco, 1989.

Crisp, Tony. *Dream Dictionary: An A to Z Guide to Understanding Your Unconscious Mind*. New York: Dell, 2002.

DeVries, Ad. *Dictionary of Symbols and Imagery*. New York: Elsevier, 1984.

Jung, C. G. *The Collected Works of C. G. Jung*. 20 vols. Princeton, N.J.: Princeton University Press, 1956–1969.

Mantoon, Mary Ann. *Understanding Dreams*. Woodstock, Conn.: Spring, 1984.

Schoenewolf, Gerald. *A Dictionary of Dream Interpretation*. Northvale, N.J.: Aronson, 1997.

Chapter Six

Barrett, Deirdre, ed. *Trauma and Dreams*. Cambridge, Mass.: Harvard University Press, 1996.

Bulkeley, Kelly. *Dreams of Healing: Transforming Nightmares into Visions of Hope*. Mahwah, N.J.: Paulist Press, 2003.

Crisp, Tony. *Dream Dictionary: An A to Z Guide to Understanding Your Unconscious Mind*. New York: Dell, 2002.

DeVries, Ad. *Dictionary of Symbols and Imagery*. New York: Elsevier, 1984.

Franz, Marie-Louise von. *On Dreams and Death*. Chicago: Open Court, 1998.

Jung, C. G. *The Collected Works of C. G. Jung*. 20 vols. Princeton, N.J.: Princeton University Press, 1956–1969.

Kalsched, Donald. *The Inner World of Trauma: Archetypal Defenses of the Personal Spirit*. New York: Routledge, 1996.

Mattoon, Mary Ann. *Understanding Dreams*. Woodstock, Conn.: Spring, 1984.

Rando, Therese A. *How to Go on Living When Someone You Love Dies*. New York: Bantam Books, 1988.

Sanford, John. *Dreams and Healing*. Mahwah, N.J.: Paulist Press, 1979.

Schoenewolf, Gerald. *A Dictionary of Dream Interpretation*. Northvale, N.J.: Aronson, 1997.

Chapter Seven

Bletzer, June G. *Encyclopedic Psychic Dictionary*. 3rd ed. Lithia Springs, Ga: New Leaf, 1998.

Bosnak, Robert. *Tracks in the Wilderness of Dreaming: Exploring Interior Landscape Through Practical Dreamwork*. New York: Delta Books, 1996.

Browne, Sylvia. *Sylvia Browne's Book of Dreams*. New York: Signet Books, 2003.

Brylowski, A. "Nightmares in Crises: Clinical Applications of Lucid Dreamers." *Psychiatric Journal of the University of Ottawa* 15 (1990): 79–84.

Cirlot, J. E. *A Dictionary of Symbols*. 2nd ed. New York: Philosophical Library, 1971.

Crisp, Tony. *Dream Dictionary: An A to Z Guide to Understanding Your Unconscious Mind*. New York: Dell, 2002.

DeVries, Ad. *Dictionary of Symbols and Imagery*. New York: Elsevier, 1984.

Edward, John. *One Last Time: A Medium Speaks to Those Who Have Loved and Lost*. New York: Berkley, 2000.

Edward, John. *After Life: Answers from the Other Side*. New York: Princess Books, 2003.

Halliday, G. "Direct Alteration of a Traumatic Nightmare." *Perceptual and Motor Skills* 54 (1982): 413–414.

Halliday, G. "Lucid Dreaming: Use in Nightmares and Sleep-Wake Confusion." In J. Gackenbach and S. LaBerge, eds. *Conscious Mind, Sleeping Brain: Perspectives on Lucid Dreaming*. New York: Plenum, 1988.

Jung, C. G. *The Collected Works of C. G. Jung*. 20 vols. Princeton, N.J.: Princeton University Press, 1956–1969.

Robinson, Lady Stearn, and Tom Corbett. *The Dreamer's Dictionary*. New York: Warner Books, 1974.

Roob, Alexander. *Alchemy and Mysticism: The Hermetic Museum*. New York: Taschen, 1997.

Shepard, Leslie A., ed. *Encyclopedia of Occultism and Parapsychology*. Detroit: Gale Research, 1991.

Taylor, Jeremy. *Dreamwork*. Mahwah, N.J.: Paulist Press, 1983.

Tholey, P. "Techniques for Inducing and Manipulating Lucid Dreams." *Perceptual and Motor Skills* 57 (1983): 79–90.

Tholey, P. "A Model for Lucidity Training as a Means of Self-Healing and Psychological Growth." In J. Glackenback and S. LaBerge, eds. *Conscious Mind, Sleeping Brain: Perspectives on Lucid Dreaming*. New York: Plenum, 1988.

Ullman, Montague, Stanley Krippner, and Alan Vaughn. *Dream Telepathy: Experiments in Nocturnal Extrasensory Perception*. 2nd ed. Jefferson, N.C.: McFarland, 1989.

Van Praagh, James. *Healing Grief: Reclaiming Life After Loss*. New York: NAL/Dutton, 2000.

Zadra, A. L. "Lucid Dreaming, Dream Control, and the Treatment of Nightmares." Paper presented at the seventh annual conference for the Association for the Study of Dreams, Chicago, June 26–30.

Chapter Eight

Alter, Robert. *The Art of Biblical Narrative*. New York: Basic Books, 1981.

Armstrong, Karen. *A History of God*. New York: Knopf, 1993.

Attig, Thomas. *How We Grieve: Relearning the World*. New York: Oxford University Press, 1996.

Aycock, Don. M. *Prayer 101: What It Is, What It Isn't, How to Do It*. Nashville, Tenn.: Broadman and Holman, 1998.

Blumenthal, David R. *Facing the Abusing God*. Louisville, Ky.: Westminster John Knox, 1993.

Breathnach, Sarah Ban. *Simple Abundance*. New York: Warner Books, 1998.

Bright, John. *The Kingdom of God*. Nashville, Tenn.: Abingdon Press, 1953.

Campbell, Joseph, with Bill Moyers. *The Power of Myth*. New York: Doubleday, 1988.

Jung, C. G. *Modern Man in Search of a Soul*. New York: Harcourt Brace, 1933.

Jung, C. G. *The Collected Works of C. G. Jung*. 20 vols. Princeton, N.J.: Princeton University Press, 1956–1969.

Kelsey, Morton. *God, Dreams, and Revelation: A Christian Interpretation of Dreams*. Minneapolis: Augsburg Fortress, 1974.

Kreeft, Peter. *Three Philosophies of Life: Ecclesiastes, Life as Vanity Job, Life as Suffering Song of Songs, Life as Love*. San Francisco: Ignatius Press, 1989.

Kushner, Harold S. *When Bad Things Happen to Good People*. New York: Avon, 1981.

Lewis, C. S. *A Grief Observed*. New York: Bantam Books, 1983.

Mosley, Glenn, and Joanna Hill. *The Power of Prayer Around the World*. Radnor, Penn.: Templeton Foundation Press, 2000.

O'Connor, Peter. *Dreams and the Search for Meaning*. Mahwah, N.J.: Paulist Press, 1987.

O'Flaherty, Wendy Doniger. *Dreams, Illusion, and Other Realities*. Chicago: University of Chicago Press, 1984.

O'Malley, William. *God: The Oldest Question*. Chicago: Loyola Press, 2000.

Postema, Don. *Space for God: The Study and Practice of Prayer and Spirituality*. Grand Rapids, Mich.: CRC Publications, 1997.

Ricouer, Paul. *The Symbolism of Evil*. Boston: Beacon Press, 1967.

Sanford, John. *Dreams and Healing*. Mahwah, N.J.: Paulist Press, 1979.

Sharpe, Jonathan. *Divining Your Dreams: How the Ancient Mystical Tradition of the Kabbalah Can Help You Interpret More Than 850 Powerful Dream Images*. New York: Simon & Schuster, 2002.

Steinpach, Richard. *Why We Live After Death*. Gambier, Ohio: Grail Foundation Press, 1979.

Taylor, Jeremy. *Dreamwork*. Mahwah, N.J.: Paulist Press, 1983.

Tedlock, Barbara, ed. *Dreaming: Anthropological and Psychological Interpretations*. New York: Cambridge University Press, 1987.

Chapter Nine

Cirlot, J. E. *A Dictionary of Symbols*. 2nd ed. New York: Philosophical Library, 1971.

Crisp, Tony. *Dream Dictionary: An A to Z Guide to Understanding Your Unconscious Mind*. New York: Dell, 2002.

DeVries, Ad. *Dictionary of Symbols and Imagery*. New York: Elsevier, 1984.

Diagnostic and Statistical Manual of Mental Disorders, Fourth Edition. Washington, D.C.: American Psychiatric Association, 1994.

Fauman, Michael. *Study Guide to Diagnostic and Statistical Manual of Mental Disorders, Fourth Edition*. Washington, D.C.: American Psychiatric Press, 1994.

Jung, C. G. *The Collected Works of C. G. Jung*. 20 vols. Princeton, N.J.: Princeton University Press, 1956–1969.

Jung, C. G. *Memories, Dreams, Reflections*. New York: Random House, 1961.

Mattoon, Mary Ann. *Understanding Dreams*. Woodstock, Conn.: Spring, 1984.

O'Connor, Peter. *Dreams and the Search for Meaning*. Mahwah, N.J.: Paulist Press, 1987.

Rando, Therese A. *How to Go on Living When Someone You Love Dies*. New York: Bantam Books, 1988.

Samuel, Andrew, Bani Shorter, and Alfred Plaut. *A Critical Dictionary of Jungian Analysis*. New York: Routledge, 1986.

Sanford, John. *Dreams and Healing*. Mahwah, N.J.: Paulist Press, 1979.

Schoenewolf, Gerald. *A Dictionary of Dream Interpretation*. Northvale, N.J.: Aronson, 1997.

Stein, Murray. *Jungian Analysis*. Boston: Shambhala, 1984.

Taylor, Humphrey. "The Religious and Other Beliefs of Americans 2003."
[www.harrisinteractive.com/harris_poll /index.asp?PID=359]. Harris Poll
Number 11, February 26, 2003.

About the Authors

Dr. T. J. Wray is assistant professor of religious studies at Salve Regina University in Newport, Rhode Island, and the author of *Surviving the Death of a Sibling: Living Through Grief When an Adult Brother or Sister Dies*. She is the creator of www.adultsiblinggrief.com and www.griefdreams.com. She is a member of the Association for the Study of Dreams and the Association for Death Education and Counseling. She lives in Rhode Island with her husband, three children, and dogs.

Ann Back Price is a Jungian psychoanalyst and clinical teaching associate in the Department of Psychiatry and Human Behavior at Brown Medical School. She is a member of the Association for the Study of Dreams and the International Association of Analytical Psychology. She lives in Rhode Island with her husband, Larry, her daughter, Laura, her son, Max, and her dog, Happy.